GRASS IS GOLD

GRASS IS GOLD

A BIOGRAPHICAL HISTORY

By

THELMA KAY MILLER

THE CHRISTOPHER PUBLISHING HOUSE
NORTH QUINCY, MASSACHUSETTS

PRINTED IN

THE UNITED STATES OF AMERICA

The scent of wild roses on the high banks and fennel in the swales takes my mother's thoughts back to her childhood as we travel the rambling roads, that spurn the shorter ways, through the Palouse hills.

She thinks then beyond the scope of memory to the things at hand and a future on this land. To her this book is dedicated with love and affection.

ACKNOWLEDGEMENTS

I wish to acknowledge the following persons and sources for their valuable assistance in compiling the information for this book.

Whitman County Agriculture Data Series, 1965, Donald W. Moos, Director, Harry C. Trelogan, Statistical Reporter, Washington Crop and Statistical Livestock Reporting Service, Seattle, Washington.

Tape Recordings from Newspapers of Colfax, Tabor Lafollette, Chairman of the History Committee.

National Archives, Washington, D.C.; Folk Art of Rural Pennsylvania, Francis Lichten; Whitman County Court House Records; *Colfax Gazette.*

"Whitman County Ports," Whitman County Port Commission, Colfax, Washington.

"Lower Snake River Dams," Brochure, U.S. Army Engineer District, Walla Walla, Washington, Corps of Engineers.

In addition, I wish to gratefully acknowledge and express my appreciation for the pictures and maps contributed by friends and relatives.

Elmer McCully, Almota, Washington; Nettie Eggers, Colfax, Washington; Mrs. Colby Harper, Porterville, California; Verna Fincher, Spokane, Washington; John Laughlin, County Tyrone, Ireland; Earl Kennel, Colfax, Washington; Doris Spillman Miller, Washington, D.C.; Sara Beth Hunsinger Roe, Kingston, Pennsylvania; Neal Klemgard, Colfax, Washington; and Bill Walters, Colfax, Washington.

PREFACE

The economic history of the Palouse is characterized by a change from grassland and livestock production to one of the richest and most productive commercially-farmed wheatlands in the United States. The Palouse is a crescent-shaped formation of five million acres of loose, spongy, volcanic soil. Perhaps originating from the once active volcanoes of the Cascades, the soil was wind and stream-deposited to a depth of twenty-five feet over the lava flows in four soil series—Ritzville, Walla Walla, Athena and Palouse. The deep topsoil, moisture absorbant and free from gravel, stone and clay, is rich in calcium and other soluble minerals due to the humus of the surface layers formed under semi-arid grasslands. These grasslands are still evident for eighty-two miles on the brakes of the Snake River and the eyebrows on the northeast slopes, where they have not been plowed out.

The large dunes have been reshaped into an intricate pattern of low rounded hills by the Palouse River and its tributaries, the Union Flat and Rebel Flat Creeks, paralleled by the Snake River, Little and the Big Penawawa Creeks, and the Latah.

As my thoughts turn back the hands of time and light the glowing lamp of memory, I dream of the moments of joy and happiness that will be forever fine.

Into the fabric of my memory have been woven many other threads of purest gold—the diminishing chill of the land in the spring, the crunching wagon wheels that munched on the weeds in the dusty road, the leathery odor of horses pulling

9

their load, the scolding zephyrs in the timber culture trees, the rhythm of the fence posts that came striding down the hill, the smell of the air inside the old root cellar and the scraping of the draft in the stovepipe being turned by hand.

Recalling the little things we loved so much in our childhood, Maida Templeton Harrison and I have spent many gratifying hours talking about the inconstant sunshine of our lives, now shredded with strands of silver tears.

TABLE OF CONTENTS

11

CAPTIONS TO ILLUSTRATIONS

1. Grovernor Comstock King, grandson of Captain Richard King of Kingsville, Texas, came as a boy of seventeen to the Penawawa Bar with his half-brothers, Lincoln Adams (left and James Adams (right). His sister, Luella King, continued on with the Adams family to the Four-Mile near Pullman, Washington. He stayed with the Emsley Fincher family and earned money to help buy food for his mother's family.

Although as a young man he came to own 1600 acres of land, he occasionally impetuously put aside his quest for wealth by plowing a curved furrow to "break out" the sod for the planting of wheat and took incredulous delight in yielding to the longing in his heart to climb and explore the longest mountain trail that beckoned along a trout filled stream and limn a deer emerging from the sheltering tall pines beside a mirrored lake.

2. In the remote distance, at the bend of the cliff road, the Fincher's delighted in their home snuggled beneath the cleft in the ledge and the good things in life. This life-like picture of the Penawawa bar was taken by Elmer McCully.

3. Nestled in the deep Snake River canyon, Penawawa, recorded April 29, 1877 by L. V. Bragg, Auditor of Whitman County, Washington, and platted November 28, 1877 by Emsley Fincher and C. C. Cram, was a haven of rest for the weary travelers who crossed on the ferry.

4. Shadows were lengthening and the after dinner lull had settled over the place when Colby Harper, a grandson, thought of taking a picture of Lura Stevenson Harper, Mary Roub Fincher, Emsley Fincher and Napoleon Cota. Lura was helping Grandmother Mary cook for the fruit crew.

13

5. With black smoke rolling from her stack, rhythmic stern-wheel turning fast and a throbbing-panting engine pushing her heavy tow up the gurgling, splashing Snake River, the *Lewiston* whistled a blast to warn that she was approaching the landing at Penawawa, Washington.

6. Thrilled by the pulling in of the salmon ensnared in the purse seign, George Rowell, Hexie Eggers and Gird Garland bend to catch deeper into the net and the muscles of their brawny arms bulge as they loop the net over the boat on the Snake River.

7. Living in a tent at the river's edge, Ed Swift was giving day and night ferry service at Penawawa, in 1918, when two escapees demanded passage. When he refused to take them across, they took over his boat. Then they failed to angle into the current properly, snapped the cable, and lodged the boat irretrievably on the rocky bank downstream.

8. A cooling, soft wind billows the protective canvasses of the "Old Holt Combine" as men of faith reap their golden wheat that others may eat. After its yield is stored, the wheat field will be a brown carpet until spring. Will Miller, Lute Templeton, Orin Martin, John Miller and Phil Miller rest from their labors at intervals.

9. Through the deep, beautiful and strong standing wheat, the thirty-two head team, with "Rocks" in the lead, pulled the ground power combine. Out of its yellow husk each grain of wheat went into the sack to help make a bushel. The dusty, strawy smell drifting from the dumps was a sure sign that the harvest had been great.

10. The tortured trees were turning red and gold as over the winding roads from these abundant, quiet farms with rolling hills, John and Will Miller hauled the seeds, each with food at its core, from the rich fields of grain. The beauty of their purpose gripped their souls and filled them with serenity.

11. Raindrops glisten on the nodding clover around the secure old house, whose windows have felt the pelting hail and smear of resinous popular bloom. The red-orange leaves of the Japanese Barberry drift across the steps and the clish of pebbles on the drive tells that someone is approaching.

12. Under a cloudless sky the barley, bordering the swerving road that helps make up the 1,982.09 miles of road in Whitman County, was burned and shattered. The very meanness of the land and weather holds us captive forever. Oliver King Miller, owner, and Dave Baldwin—custom operator.

13. In 1968, this self-propelled, John Deere 95-H, owned by Dave Baldwin and operated by Clarence Braman, moves slowly but surely through the rustling, murmuring wheat. It cuts, threshes and elevates it into the bulk trucks to be hauled to the Colfax Grain Grower's Elevator at Penawawa, Washington.

14. Like wheat ripened in the bright sunshine, the graceful stalks form a four-cornered arch over the head of the lady fair whose lively green skirt drapes all around over the gold ball of beauty. Long white gloves give Darlene Wright of Fairfield, Washington, a sophisticated air. A tantalizing flavor spirals from the golden crusted loaf of bread on the circular table.

15. Whitman Community Hospital (dedicated Sunday, November 3, 1968 at 2:00 p.m.) has, among other special equipment, an Amsco steam sterilizer, chamber volume of five cubic feet; a $3,000. anesthesia machine; X-ray for fluoroscoping and Radiographic examination; a $2,000. cryostat for prompt diagnosis of cancer and a $2,000. Hampton Shampaine Obstetrical Table.

16. On October 28, 1969, President Lyndon Johnson gave an executive order to the Corps of Engineers to build a cofferdam around the Marmes Man Shelter. The Rock Shelter and diggings has been designated a National Historic Landmark site by the National Park Service. It was named for the man who owned

the ranch where it was discovered, Roland J. Marmes. It is the richest diggings for bones of the oldest man that has been found on this continent. Skeletal remains of four ancient Indians have been unearthed along with missile points. The second bone needle has been found showing that these men who lived 11,000 to 13,000 years ago had the intelligence to sew together small animal skins to make body coverings. These men stopped for shelter in the basalt depression high above the Palouse River, 15 miles southeast of Washtucna, and a mile upstream from the Snake River where the Lower Monumental Dam is being constructed. Some charred bone fragments may be the fourth skeletal remains found at the site. A 8½ inch long spear point, 8,000 years old and made of basalt, was also found.

ENNEWAYA CITY.

NOVEMBER 28 1877

TS 8   IN SEC 15 TIAN RA1E

for

EMSLEY FINCHER

AND

C. C. CRAM

Scale 200 ft to an inch

3

4   18

7

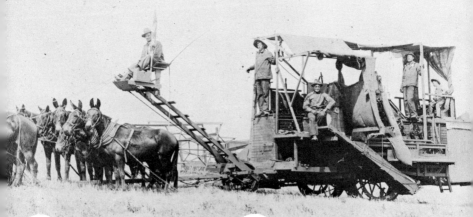

8

20

13

23

14

15

16

PALOUSE RIVER

MARMES
ROCK SHELTER

24

NS FERRY

Mary, a very tiny woman, was as quick as thought. She bustled around the house sewing on the buttons that came off, catching up the freyed hemlines and polishing the tableboards. Her calico dresses had skirts pleated to a belt that opened by a placket on the side; pleated waist fronts. Most of her basques had a high collar and long gathered sleeves. Some of her Sunday dresses had a lay back collar with a ruffled trim or maybe a row of beads on taffeta.

She wore a cape instead of a coat. It went down to the waist and tied in front with a ribbon, and had scrolls of beads on it. Her buttoned shoes had medium to low heels. The buttons on these shoes were small, round and black.

For work in the orchards, Emsley wore shirts of blue-gray gingham and heavy work shoes that laced. His Sunday shirt was made of black satin and he wore "Bluchers"—two-pieced soft leather shoes that didn't have any seams. The heel part came to the front and laced.

"Come and let me cut your hair," contrived Mary. "Then I'll shave your cheeks and eyebrows." She insisted that he be neat.

"Ira, Henry, Owen and Johnny are ditching the water from the upper spring down past the house, across the road and into the field below with hoes. Katie wants to carry the willow switches in her apron while the boys plant them along the irrigating ditch," she said. "Billy Webster will tell the boys how to do it!" she concluded.

As soon as the ground had mellowed after plowing it with a foot-burner—a single-bladed plow—Emsley bought the old Malta, Salloway and Elberta peaches from May's nursery in Walla Walla for the orchard between the road that went to the house and the one that turned west. Apple and peach orchards above and below the road were irrigated from the north spring.

Between the peach orchard and the road that went up past

the warm spring and up the Fincher grade, he planted a vineyard of Muscatel and sweet water grapes. The water that
flowed down into the vineyard and into the garden, where
they grew potatoes, peanuts, corn and tomatoes, came from
up higher in the gulch above the warm spring. This spring
was warm enough so that during the winter a vapor hovered
over it. It was ditched into the cherry orchard beyond Rattlesnake Bluff.

After threshing out a few peanuts, digging new potatoes
and starting to pick the few tomatoes that had ripened for
her family's dinner, Mary shrieked, "Come kill this snake!
I've been bitten!" She was choking with excitement and had
excruciating pain in her left wrist, which had two long cuts
across it. After drawing blood from the wound and putting it
in a mudpack, they obtained whiskey from the men on the
steamboat and gave her as much as she could take. Two white
scars always reminded her not to put her hand in any hidden
place.

While the Fincher house was being started in 1873, Charlie
Cram was finishing the setting up of the Penawawa Ferry,
initiated in 1872. "Anchor the steel cable in the solid rock on
the Garfield County side," he told his son, Henry. "On the
Whitman County side I will build a high scaffolding and run
the steel cable through the top of it, securing the end of the
cable by winding it around some huge rocks and burying them
in the ground. Begin by threading the cable through the eye
of this long iron rod which will fasten to the ferryboat," rasped
Charlie. "Tie two large knots in the ends of the cable so they
will not slip through the eye."

Contingent upon the construction of the road past the
Fincher place to Union Flat and from the Snake River to
Pohata, Emsley consented to sell Charlie land for a townsite,
on both sides of the road where it left the river, for a sum of
sixty dollars.

"Plot a town," entreated Emsley, one of the two first permanent residents.

"Mr. Byrd will help with the drawing of the plots and naming the streets. Have it recorded by A. L. Knowlton at Colfax while it is still 1877."

Thus, Penawawa, tucked close to the river by towering bluffs, was soon shaded by trees, and the loving care lavished on their homes by the people made it beautiful.

There was a building about twelve by twenty feet, with a front and back door and no porches, that had counters and shelves inside. It was a general merchandise store fabricated on the left side of the street, and opened by Elliott and Andress.

"Emma, Anna and Katie, go to the store and get me a pound of flour, sugar, beans and coffee," said Mary. "Your father likes oyster casserole so bring two cans of oysters and a box of crackers. We have enough salt, pepper and fresh butter. I will bring pickles up from the cellar. You may stop at Mrs. Sparks and see her beautiful white angora cats with pink eyes if you don't stay too long."

Across the street from the store, a two-story building partitioned into five bedrooms, a spacious living room, dining room and kitchen was the hotel.

To accommodate the people who crossed on the ferry, Tom Simpson erected a triangular livery stable with a loft for baled hay. Penawawa was the crossing on the old territorial road where families emigrating into the Palouse grassland stopped to feed their animals and rest before continuing on their trek.

For storing wool, fruit and grain, waiting to go out on the steamboats, a warehouse was constructed on the east side of Main Street by the Hawley Dodd Co., in 1878, which competed with Mr. Cram's warehouse, built in 1873. The roof of the Hawley Dodd Co. warehouse was twisted and scattered for one-half mile by a cyclone in 1882.

On the left side of Third Street was the school. It was white with windows along one side and no steps; you could walk right in.

With a sulky plow, a two-bottom, with a little square seat that he sat on, Emsley was plowing the orchards early in the spring. He now owned five hundred and thirty acres of sandy-loam soil that, because of its six-hundred and thirteen-foot elevation, was ideal for fruit growing. Blossoms were falling like sifting snow.

"Owen and Johnny, hoe around the trees to get the weeds out," said Emsley at breakfast. "We'll prune before the sap comes up, and re-ditch."

"Put the water on the trees before it gets warm and keep it on them until the fruit is ripe and ready to pick," reminded Mary.

"Some of the fruit must be taken off so the rest will mature," continued Emsley.

"On a quiet, clear day, using the big tank and the wagon, we are going to spray for worms, aphids and scale. Owen and Johnny can carry the hose around the tree while I operate the pump."

Every day during the summer, eighteen to twenty rigs came to Emsley's orchards as the fruit ripened—cherries, peaches, prunes, plums, berries, pears and apples.

Mary put the weighing scales, with cross bars and weights, under the cherry tree at the end of the porch.

"I'll weigh your fruit," she told him as he came from the orchard. "Soft fruit goes back in the extra baskets for sauce if you want to take it," explained Mary, as she reached for a basket.

Heart racing, face flushed, eyes dilated and hands shaking, she scrambled into William Gordon's wagon, round coiled the snake striking his length each time until he wriggled into the irrigating ditch.

"Mother has fainted," called Owen from the orchard.

"Johnny! Come and help me carry her into the house."

"Emma, fix a hops and vinegar poultice while Anna bathes the cold sweat from her face," he panted.

"I must have been fear-struck," muttered Mary.

"Aunt Mary, Melvin Crumbaker is coming to install our telephone," interjected Roy Jones.

When he had finished fastening the dry-cell battery phone to the wall and connecting it to the fence, Mr. Crumbaker said, "Now you children can call your neighbors for help."

"Who could we call?" asked Anna.

"The Colfax exchange is already serving more than twenty-five phones," said Melvin.

"Call Cassy Jones, your mother, and ask her to come down for a few days," said Emma.

Roy called his mother and everyone took a turn talking to her.

"The prune drier is ready to unpack, mother, so I must get busy," he told her.

Roy Jones ran the prune drier. Washed and pitted prunes were laid on the trays, pit side up, on the outside of the building and shoved into the racks on either side. The fire was built on the cement floor under the metal shield to keep the temperature right. After several days the dried fruit was packaged in brown sacks or wooden boxes.

CHAPTER II

UP ON TOP OF THE HILL

Ira and Henry were herding their father's sheep on the hills back of the rim rock as far east as the Templeton place on the Penawawa Creek, and as far north as Tubbs Spring from across the old Michaelson place on Alkali Flat.

A band of sheep had just watered at the spring, so Ira and Henry had to wait for the spring to fill up. They sat down to rest before climbing the slope where their sheep were grazing.

Bleating sheep came lunging down the slope toward the spring. Over the knoll, Ira and Henry found the white face of one of their grass-fed animals blobbed with blood and with its hindquarters torn and bleeding. A coyote had sneaked in.

"Hike! Hike" ripped out Ira.

"Go get them Tag," boomed Henry. "Mage, bring them in!"

Ira and Henry "flocked up" the sheep and after they were watered drove them to the brakes of the Snake River.

"Henry, you can sleep in our tented wagon tonight," offered Ira. "I'll watch the sheep to see that they do not leave the bedding grounds."

"Ya, ho!" echoed and re-echoed across the ravine.

"Ya, ho!" returned Henry.

"I am bringing an aide to camp," disclosed Emsley. "Grovernor King is going to stay with us and help herd through the day so the night watchman can sleep."

Three years had passed before Grovernor King and Katie Fincher, bedazzled by being in love—awed, thrilled, frightened

47

and elated—watched the oscillating stars beat down upon them, the silver of a moon slide across the sky, turning leaves flash silver in their quiet sleep, and listened to the water rushing by.

"Oh, come on," wheedled Grovy holding her hands in his. "I'll hitch up the team early in the morning and meet you down at the gate. We'll go to Moscow and get married."

"I'll be there," assured Katie smiling coyly.

Gentle-mannered Grovy, pure of heart and keen of eye, looked very debonair in a white shirt, plaid tie, buttoned vest, wide-lapelled coat and a straight-brimmed hat. His winning smile reflected the boy's worthiness. In a blue taffeta dress, that had a long jacket with a smocked front, panelled and shirred skirt caught up in front with a ribbon bow and a lace collar and cuffs, Katie challenged the eye of her lover. A ribbon run through her straw hat formed a half-crown accented by a cluster of roses.

The small town of Penawawa, in this secluded spot, was silent in the early May morning. They were not conscious of the strain of everyday living. From Penawawa, Grovy and Katie blissfully drove to Moscow, Idaho on May 13, 1881, and were married. Coming back as far as the home of Grovy's mother on the Four Mile, they stayed all night.

After the excitement and gaiety of their trip, the event of their marriage seemed very real. Johnny, her brother, met them on the five-mile bar where the road wrenches away to the left and ends abruptly at the landing. Johnny took Emsley's team and hack home. Grovy and Katie took a boat over to the Rice bar. They spent a very enjoyable week with the Rice family.

"You and Katie take my boat and I will be over for it, Grovy," offered Mr. Rice. "Look at the ripples spreading from the center and circling into nothingness."

"Remember, Grovy, not to stand up in the boat!"

The reprimand stung the brawny young man as he put the oars into the skiff and slid it into the water. Enthralled by the sense of skimming through the water, they did not notice the seepage in the bottom of the boat. Suddenly, cold fear came over him. He sat with oars frozen. Then with a quick maneuver he dropped the oars and frantically helped dip the water out, until the skiff swirled into the drift along the west shore above the fish weirs.

"My throat feels like sandpaper," managed Katie, pluckily sitting on thorns. The sun, falling on the water, had flushed her face and her hands were fluttering above her head. In the bottom of the rented boat, elongated heads of baby rattlesnakes were appearing.

"Maybe we can get a drink at Pangburn's," suggested Grovy.

They climbed out and tied the boat. When they got to Pangburn's, Alice was anxious to go with them so they all walked to the Fincher's.

Along the road from the gate, flowering cherry trees were thrust against the blue sky. Their pink blossoms covered the ground and their fragrance filled the air. Climbing honeysuckles circled the porch posts. Hyacinths and narcissus banked by hens and chickens skirted the porch.

The hard-muscled figure with heavy beard and monumental brows—Emsley Fincher—appeared in the door as Grovy, Katie and Alice came toward the house.

"Alice, you can come in but Grovy and Katie stay out!" wrathfully scolded Emsley.

Grovy looked askance at Katie. They both gaped at him in astonishment and then Katie said stiffly, "Very well, Father, we will go away." With a defiant toss of her head, she turned and was going down the path when Emsley called them back.

Mary put her arms around her daughter's neck and Grovy's.

He had been good with the sheep and had earned a band of three-hundred head of his own.

She said, "You know Grovy about the little boy who fell down—he got up and walked right on again. Next time you children need to borrow the team, ask your father. Come now and eat your dinner."

Her name was Fanny. She was an Australian Shepherd, a sheep dog, with a black muzzle, long shaggy coat, floppy ears and a snip in the face. She was barking under the porch.

"What is making her bark?" speculated Owen at dinner.

"She might have puppies under the porch!" ventured Johnny.

"Come on, Johnny," demanded Owen. With panic washing over him at the thought of losing the puppies, he pulled back from the table and rushed outside followed by Johnny and Emsley.

This was the day Emsley bluffed a four-foot diamondback rattlesnake, the most dangerous snake in the world.

The western rattler had come down from his sun-baked home on the rocky bluff during the night to search for food.

"He'll rest in the shade until sundown. Then he will feed on the puppies," explained Emsley. "Owen bring me a lantern! Henry, bring me the kerosene!"

Emsley put the lantern near the puppies saying, "He will not come toward the light."

"Can you see his eyes glisten?"

"What are we going to do, Father?"

"We will take the boards off the porch floor and put the puppies in the basket where Fanny sleeps.

Round coiled the snake, when the board above it was lifted, striking the four-foot length of its body plus about two and one-half feet down the hill before Emsley cut its head off with the hoe. This western diamondback had shed his skin six times as indicated by the rattlers on his tail. His keeled scales formed diamonds along his back that were white-edged and shone in the sun.

Grovy King went to Colfax with the wagon and loaded it with windows and lumber for the building of a house on the Jack Melroy place. He started home and was nearing the Alec Canutt home, father of Yakima Canutt, when one horse fell over the bank because he got scared and pulled the other horse and wagon after him. The windows and lumber were all thrown across the creek and broken into splinters, and so he and Katie moved into the small house built by Jack Melroy. I was born in this house about two miles "up on the hill," north of Grandfather Emsley Fincher's place at Pena-wawa, in 1885.

The deep sorrow of losing Floyd Loren King, his first child, had changed my father's life. That summer he hauled wheat to be shipped out on the steamboats at Almota from the Matt Johnson place. He was paymaster for the crew on the railroad line from Colfax to Pullman, Washington in the early fall.

"Do you have a baby in this camp?" one of the men asked when the crew came the last time for their pay. "We never heard her before."

"She was here when you came," my mother explained.

After the railroad was cut through, the big granite rocks above the Grogan Hodge place were cut and hauled by rail to Pullman to build the Methodist Church.

My father traded the Jack Melroy quarter for the one that joined it, the Cota place. Then he came in possession of what is now known as the Henry Krom, Sr. ranch on Alkali Flat. Before we moved to the Tubbs Spring quarter, that cornered with the Henry Krom place, my father sold our band of sheep. It is assumed that Hiram Tubbs owned this quarter before moving to the Wayne Major place in-so-far as the spring and quarter were named after him.[2]

Our home, where our souls were at peace, had four rooms and a front porch. There were two front doors. One opened into the living room and one opened into the kitchen. You could go into the two bedrooms from the living room or kitchen. We had a nice cellar to the side of the house that had about two feet of dirt on top of it. We carried water from the well behind the house for cooking and drinking, and for watering the flowers around the front porch, which were fenced with pickets cut from the wood salvaged from the wreck of the *Annie Faxon* on the Snake River.

"We will haul wood up from the Snake River," said Pa. "You and Olive can ride on the high seat of the long-bedded wheat wagon that has the metal-tired wheels. Put the lunch in the jockey box and I'll fill the canteen with fresh water for drinking."

"We will meet you at the gate," laughed Katie.

We traveled along glumly until we could see the mighty and great river that Meriwether Lewis and William Clark passed down, in 1805. Pa stopped the team and we sat on the rocky hillside, peering into the deep canyon at the tortuous waters of the river that seemed to be savagely thrusting itself against its outer banks with a mighty sweep.

"Do you know where the Snake River rises, Katie?" queried Grovy.

"Somewhere in the North?" she guessed.

---

2 This was the pastorial stage of agricultural development in the Palouse country. People depended on their herds and flocks. If one quarter of land did not afford good pasture, they moved to another, often trading animals for the land. Grass was their primary form of food. Cattle, sheep, horses and chickens ate the grass and nourished the people by providing them with meat, milk and eggs. From the cereal grains they made flour and the sheep gave them wool for clothing, mattresses and rugs. Grass populated the Palouse.

"It rises clean and clear in the Teton Mountains in Wyoming and loops like a snake's track through Wyoming, Idaho, Oregon and Washington. The fur traders named it 'the Snake' because of the Snake tribe of Indians that lived along its banks," offered Grovy.

"It surely has cut a deep canyon," remarked Katie, when they had neared the bottom of the grade.

"The Grand Canyon of the Snake River is the world's deepest gorge," said Grovy. "It averages 6,600 feet in depth and the width varies from four to nine miles in Hell's Canyon."

When we got to the main street in Penawawa, we met a host of fishermen coming up from the landing. They had been whipping the stream since dawn. Most of them had fish in their creels. We drove to the end of the street and down by the drift.

Nelson Cota had a boat tied in by the ferry landing and he and Papa went out in the boat with cant hooks to bring in a log that didn't seem to have any branches on it. When they put their hooks into the log, it turned and the branch that was attached to the underside came up under the boat and upset it.

Uncle Cota was an excellent swimmer and he managed to turn the boat and help Papa back into it. They lost their cant hooks so we picked up what wood had come into the drift. I was getting tired before the wagon was full, so I climbed up in the seat to go to sleep. However, before falling asleep, I looked up the river and saw a house coming down.

"There's a house coming down the river," I shouted, but they didn't pay any attention.

"Mama, come and see the house," I chortled, pointing with first one hand and then the other.

It took the house quite a little while to come down from the long hollow, across the rapids, so they could see it.

"Look at the man in the rowboat. He is turning the house

in the current," said Uncle Cota. "Shall we go out and help him, Grovy?"

"Something, like a piano, is making one corner go deep into the water. We couldn't beach it without hooks!" protested Grovy. They didn't row out there and the house full of furniture went to Riparia and broke up on the railroad bridge.

We stopped by Grandmother Mary Fincher's house, and she was not expecting us. She took a pan of feed from the log cabin and called her chickens, "Chickie, Chickie, Chickie."

She reached down and picked up a Plymouth Rock, Black Cochin and Minorcas by the legs, rung their necks and dipped them in scalding water. She cooked the chickens in a big stew kettle, made dumplings and creamed the potatoes. We had homemade bread and butter to eat with the chicken.

The Jack Warner family had come for tomatoes and after we had eaten, Grandfather Emsley said as he took out his violin, "What would you like to sing, Grovy?"

"Golden Slippers," suggested Grovy. "Jack can play one piece and you can play the next."

"Katie can sing soprano, Grovy bass, and we'll all sing," joined in Grandmother Mary.

After we had sung, "House on the Sands," "The Two Little Orphans," and many other family favorites, it was midnight and grandmother invited us to stay overnight.

When we awakened the next morning, the gumps were already chirring down in the orchards. They picked up the windfalls in the orchards besides the Kaffir corn and other chopped grains that Grandma fed them.

Grandmother made buttermilk pancakes and a delicious thin syrup for our breakfast. She gave Mama a fresh start of everlasting yeast for her bread baking and some apple butter from the big crocks upstairs.

"Olive can carry the setting of Black Cochin eggs in the lunch basket," said Katie.

When we got home, Mama put them under one of our broody hens and in about three weeks she had twelve black chicks in the nest. Mama took them from the nest and put them in a coop. The mother hen taught them to eat the crumbs and chopped grain that I poked through the slats of the coop.

"I spoke to Mrs. Michaelson about taking care of you, Katie. She said if you would put a piece of white cloth on the clothes line in the yard that she would come anytime. Nelson Cota is herding sheep west of the Tubbs Spring and he will come for me if he sees the signal. Tommy may come to our house to live any day now," said father.

And he did. Tommy, my brother, was born when my father was working away from home, in 1887.

My brother was still small when a man came to our house to get something to eat. A stranger, transient, came "riding in."

"Could you give me something to eat?" he asked.

My mother smiled and said, "Come in, sir."

He was a tall man and weighed about one hundred and eighty pounds. He was riding "Ribbon, a very small pony. She had a saddle mark around her. He offered the little mare to pay for his meals. He had come so far and the pony was very tired. He stayed several days. When he was ready to leave, he gave me a gold brooch and walked up the road out of sight. In a day or two the sheriff of Whitman County, John Echo, came to our house.

"Have you seen a tall man riding a small bay horse, Mr. King?" inquired Sheriff Echo.

"Does he have an upper lip that he draws in when he eats to keep it from coming down over his teeth?" Papa asked.

"Yes, I have a warrant for his arrest as a jewel thief. Did he leave any loot with you?"

"Yes, he gave Olive a brooch that you may have."

"He left his horse to pay for his meals. Was it stolen, too?"

"No, he owned the horse and she is yours, Mr. King," said Sheriff Echo.

Tommy and I rode "Ribbon" through the rye grass. In the muted gray-green salt grass that grew between the clumps of rye, curlews—brown, slick, and taller than the Killdeer, darted two and fro. Horned lizards—slender, rough bodies, six to seven inches long, less than an inch wide, with flat tails, and gray in color—wriggled across the dusty trails.

"Did you bring our tobacco sacks, Olive?" asked Tommy.

"You take that one and hold it over a red squirrel hole in the ground and I'll take this one," I told him. Our childish hearts had a million things to do, as the hot alkali dust blistered our feet. We trapped long enough to get our sacks full of little ones before we pulled the strings tight and put them in a large sack to take home.

The little gray owl with yellow eyes and feathered ears that stuck up was our greatest fascination. We walked around him and tried to make him turn his head off. But, of course, he was turning his head in his feathers when we couldn't see him so we never succeeded in turning the head off an owl, although we skipped wide-eyed round about.

Tommy and I were digging behind the cellar.

"Look, Olive," he said, holding up a bottle that had something in it that looked like candy.

"Tommy! Tommy! It's smoking," I screamed.

We ran to the watering trough to wash it off and in a few minutes we had the whole trough smoking. I took the bottle and dashed into the house.

"That is phosphorus! Where did you find it?" asked Mama.

"Out on the ground behind the cellar," I gulped.

Filling the bottle with water, she screwed the lid on tight and dropped it back into the hole.

"You children put the dirt into the hole and fill the woodbox," remonstrated Mama. "I'll bake bread for your father's lunch."

After she made up her yeast with one-half cup of sugar, one large tablespoon of salt, water from six or eight potatoes, and one mashed very fine, she put in the starter from the time before.

"Olive, you can bring your stool and help put the yeast in the warming oven so it will be ready in the morning."

Tommy watched us curiously.

When Papa came in from the hayfield, he said, "I traded for a new horse to ride to round-up the cattle, Katie. Prince is a big bay. I got him and another horse from John Devlin with halters for 'boot'."

"I have the haystack up, so I'll ride out and bring them in for winter feeding."

In the morning there was a skift of snow on the frozen ground. While Papa and we children were finishing our breakfast, Mama set aside one-half pint of yeast for a new starter, filled the big granite pan about half full of flour and made a hole in it. Pouring the yeast into the hole, she stirred in the flour until she had a soft dough which she put into the warming oven to raise.

"Olive, put on your leggings, and Tommy, your gloves and boots," she demanded. "We'll all go out and watch Papa saddle the new horse."

Papa buckled on his chaps and spurs.

He led the horse, saddled and bridled, from the barn. Standing near his shoulders he lifted the stirrup and swung his right leg over. Plunging, fighting and throwing himself this way and that, he came down with his legs stiff and his head between his knees. He pitched Papa, with every ounce of his strength, into the haystack. With wide nostrils, blazing eyes, breathing heavily and with feet braced, he stood trembling before swinging aside and plunging madly down the slope.

We rushed to help Papa up, but he rose to his feet abruptly and put his hat on his curly head.

"Are you hurt?" we asked eagerly.

"No," he answered curtly, with an amazed look on his face.

Mama nodded her head, understandingly, and helped him to the house. Still he hesitated to admit that the pain in his back persisted.

After fixing a turpentine and lard poultice, she said quietly, "You get right into bed and I'll apply heat to your back."

Papa fell asleep and Mama took the pone out of the warming oven. It had doubled in size. She turned it onto a floured breadboard and kneaded it down, squeezing off a portion and shaping it between her hands into a loaf. Then she rolled it over in a greased baking pan.

After putting the four large loaves in the oven she said, "Olive, you wash your hands and then you can put on your apron and roll the biscuits in this small pan."

"Tommy, keep the wood in the stove. The bread has to bake in a fairly hot oven for an hour."

When the bread was done Mama brushed the top of the loaves and biscuits with melted butter and gave each of us children a heel dipped in butter, so we didn't have to wait until supper.

As soon as Papa could ride again, he went out on Pedro and corralled the band of twenty unbroken horses from the open range. Rushing, leaping and whirling, they ground the earth in the corral into a fine dust. He cut Prince out from the maze of flying feet and tossing manes. He whirled the loop of his lasso to its length and it hit the mark. Prince plunged and tugged at the rope, as Papa was snubbing him up to a post. Papa tried to put his hand on his sweaty neck, and narrowly escaped a blow from his front hoofs. Deftly and gently he slipped the saddle blanket off. He put a thicker rope around his neck and removed the bridle with the reins almost completely trampled off.

The scrounge-mixed gray, buckskin and sorrel cayuses in the corral leaped and hurled themselves against the fence that hemmed them in until the gate that led from the corral to the open range swung open. From where Tommy and I sat on the fence we could see that one of the bays had an eighteen inch hoof on one left front foot that he threw as he ran. Papa traded Prince to Mr. Goosey who broke him by fastening half a beef on him and leading him to Colfax.

A boiling caldron of dust spread over the flat as Francis Hanna, a slight, dark, graceful rider reached the gate of our corral with the cattle branded Half-Diamond-J.

In the herd at the Long place, my father had some calves still to be branded.

"If you think Olive wouldn't get too tired she could ride over with us, Katie," said Papa.

When we got to the Snake River, I was very weary, but I stayed on high ground at a good distance while my father worked at the snubbing post.

Mr. Hanna, who had been our foreman for four years, stretched each of our calves by the heels with his lasso and tied its legs with another short rope he had snapped to his chaps.

Papa took our Half-Diamond-J branding iron from the fire and pressed it against the leg of each calf, and then returned it to the fire until all of ours were branded.

Mr. Long had a long billed magpie that would fly down and nip at the heels of the men who were working. The men wore high boots, so they would kick at the bird and he would hop over on the ground even though they did not really hit him. He was a pet on the Long Ranch.

"You can take them over to Long's feeding lot on the river, Frank," said Papa.

Sam Grady was heading his band toward the ferry at Penawawa.

When he reached the ferry Mr. Richards asked, "How many do you have?"

"They will go on all right," declared Sam.

"Well, we can try it," assented the ferryman.

When the ferryboat was about in the middle of the river, the cattle crowded to one side and caused one side of the ferryboat to go down into the water too far. Sam Grady went on the outside of the railing to drive them back, but the milling cattle all came over to his side and shoved him into the river. The last Mr. Richards saw of Sam was the whip he was still holding. Both he and the cattle were drowned. It was June and the river was bank to bank.

Mr. Richards owned the ferry and a small orchard below the Fincher slew. He had profited by jerking the hides from the thousands of head of cattle that stood for three months in the drifts without food during the "Big Freeze" in 1881. The animals licked snow for moisture and consumed the fat they had stored in their bodies. In the spring after the animals had been frozen and the sun came out, Mr. Richards started the skins off by cutting and then by hooking on and pulling he slipped them right off.

When Papa and I were nearing home, we met Elijah Hopkins.

"Some boys robbed Mr. Goosey's house at Tubbs Spring," he told us.

"How did they do it?" asked Papa.

"They went into his house and heated knives on the stove and threatened to burn his feet if he didn't get off the woodbox where he had his money hidden. They got all he had!"

"Katie is waiting for us, but we are sorry to know," my father said as we started on up the flat.

That winter we attended many dances and literaries. My

father, Grovernor Comstock King, often took care of the
dance floors. He waxed and powdered the floors. The couples
paid him at the door, $1.50 for dancing all evening. He danced
with everyone and introduced those that were strangers. A
first and second violinist played schottisches, cadrells, waltzes,
polkas and two-steps. They formed two big circles and coupled
off. The gentleman asked the lady, "May I have this dance?"
"It would be my pleasure," the lady would answer. They
danced until the late hours if it was a week night. Martin
Bostic would hold me by the fingers and we would waltz
sometimes at the "Cashup Davis" Hotel on Steptoe.

Papa played the accordian and sang tenor, Mama sang
soprano, and we children followed them on the literary programs at the Penawawa, Willow Creek and the Cram schools.
Alec Canutt arranged the debating teams for these programs.

The next summer when I was five years old I stayed with
Aunt Carrie.

"Olive, you help Uncle John dig the dirt out of the cracks
in the floor with a needle?" requested Aunt Carrie.

After working most of the day Saturday, I asked, "May I
go up to Grandma's?"

"Yes, you must be back in time for supper," said Uncle John.

I told Grandma Fincher how unhappy I was and she said,
"If Aunt Carrie is too cranky with you, you can come and
live over here."

I went down and got my clothes and went right up there.

Mama bought calico from Mr. Livingston, who canvassed
from house to house, and made pinafores for me to wear to
school. The dress I wore the first day had little pink hearts on
a white background, and my new hat set just right on top
of my head.

When the long awaited day arrived, I struggled out of bed
and dressed. Lanky, bashful Uncle Roub and I ate our breakfast and scurried down through the orchard.

School had been in session about an hour when I heard the jingling of my Dad's harness and the rumble of his wagon wheels on the road that passed the schoolhouse.

I climbed up on a desk that stood in front of the window and waved to him.

Mr. Black, the craggy-featured teacher, who had deep set eyes, a shock of iron gray hair and powerful hands, took me down and slapped my face.

"We do not leave our seats without permission, Olive," he said.

Uncle Roub came right over to me.

"That's her father," he blurted with an embarrassed smile. He took me by the hand and pulled me over to my seat. I cried, and cried, and cried.

Uncle Roub and I ran up through Grandma Fincher's orchard for dinner.

"I'm not going back to school again," he stammered.

"Why not, Roub?" asked Grandma.

He told her what happened and she said, "Olive is just beginning and you must take her back in the morning, Roub."

Of course, he had to stay too after we got to school.

Uncle Roub and I attended the Penawawa school three months during the summer of 1890 when I was five years old. He and I went to school with Nellie and Everett Jeanette, Herbert Smith, Edith Smith, Chauncey Smith, George Smith, Elmer Smith, Edna Smith, Jennie Young (the Young children came down the river in a boat from the bar), Charlie Simpson, Lloyd Rich, Abe Rich, the Blackburn boy, Leon Cota (someone hit him in the face with a rock), Alta Cota, Donnie Lee and George Lee.

The Deep Green Snake River

We love the languid river, green and slow,
Gliding past fruit ladened orchards

With branches bending low,
  And dusty harvest fields with gold aglow.
Over the basalt ledges
  And through the deep canyon it flows,
Moaning endlessly in swirling eddies
  As if stung by hate,
It takes seaward in its clutches
  Untold secrets of late.
Like a true serpent's track
  In the trail dust up from the gate,
It slithers on to lower land
  A wider stream of a faster rate,
Receiving the clear spring water
    from the rills
Swift-flowing from the breaks among the hills.

CHAPTER III

ACROSS THE RIVER

I rode on the milk wagon with the Michaelson kids to school near Dusty the next summer for three months. Anna Stinson was my teacher and then she taught in another school on Alkali Flat and I went to that school the following summer.

After the autumn leaves swirled by the wind were piling up around our house so that they rustled beneath our feet, my father planted a timber culture on the adjoining quarter of land on Alkali Flat at the Goose Hunter place.

"We are going to Colfax, Saturday," my father said, "We will stop at Aunt Emma Harper's house."

We usually traveled to town and spent the whole day doing our "trading" on Saturday. We dressed in our best Sunday clothes for going to town, and bought enough groceries to last until the next Saturday. We enjoyed visiting with our friends and neighbors in the stores and on the street.

We pulled up in front of Aunt Emma's gate, and I ran around the wagon to swing it back.

"Blow Snakes!" I panted as I clawed at the wagon.

"Puff! Puff! Puff!" The odor from the large snake in the grass wafted wide over the countryside.

"Come on, let's go on to town and stop on our way back," said Katie.

We met Ivy Harper in town and she said, "Yes, I can come and help you, Aunt Kate."

65

She stayed with us until after my brother Frank was born in 1893.[3]

To entertain ourselves while Mama and Ivy were busy, Tommy and I had a parade.

"I will take Nanny, the red Durham calf, by the ears and be the leader. You can hang onto Nanny's tail, and Sancho, the dog, and the cats will follow."

Pete Nirats going by on his way to Endicott would wave his hand and holler, "Hi, Kids, are you going to town?"

When I was eight years old, my grandmother, Martha King Adams, moved to Pullman from her ranch on the Four Mile. I stayed with her and went to school each winter until I was twelve.

She had one dress that she wore during the week.

"Bring me my lace collar, Olive," she would say. "We are going to church. You will find my pin in the cushion on my dresser."

Her collars were lace that she knitted on steel needles. She wore them to church over her everyday dress. She parted her hair in the middle and held one side in her mouth while she curled the other side around her finger and laid a curl behind her ear.

Grandmother was slight, trim and never idle. She knitted for a company in San Francisco and all the family helped her including Grandfather. She knitted doilies, center pieces, yards of lace for petticoats and bedspreads for her own home as well as for each of her children.

She taught me to set the table, saying, "Put the silver castor that I brought from Ireland in the middle of the table. It has the salt, sugar, syrup and vinegar in it. Put the knife, fork

---

3 Dusty was called Leroy. Albion was called Guy. There wasn't any town at La Cross. At Pampa there was a hotel, warehouse, railroad station, blacksmith's shop, stores, a school and several houses. The land was not broke out around Pampa.

and spoon on the right side of the plates. The extra salt and pepper go to the right of my plate, the pads for the vegetables and gravy to the left of my plate, at the head of the table. The plates for the meat and the bread go in front of Grandpa's place."

Dinner was served with love and care. She stood and passed the potatoes, gravy, cooked vegetables and raw salad to the right and let them come back to their places on the left. Grandpa passed the meat and bread. The food was always wholesome. All of the family knelt on the right side of their chairs for evening prayer. Grandfather bowed his head and our hearts were filled with gladness as our spirits, too, were fed. To help us realize our latest dreams we shared them with the family. When it was time to serve dessert, Grandma stood at the end of the table and raised her little flat hand to each member of the family saying, "What kind will you have?"

To a dinner guest she said, "Uncle Cota, have a piece of apple pie. The other kind is the best."

She told Tommy and I, "If you want to go back to Ireland with me someday, you will have to learn to eat bread."

She gave us dry bread and while we sat on the stairs eating it she would tell us about Gorticastle in North Ireland where she was born.

"Gorticastle was built by William Laughlin in 1736, a descendant of the first man in charge of the Cannon Gun of Derry in 1689. The McLaughlins were a very old Irish family, whose name goes back to King Niles who lived four hundred years after Christ. In the fifth generation of our family, William Laughlin married Jane Y. Frazer. I, Martha Matilda Laughlin, was the eighth child born to them in 1844 at Sperrin, Tyrone County, North Ireland.

"My father promised me to an old man to be his bride when I was sixteen. Brother John sent me the money to come to mother's people in Philadelphia. Sister Mary was married and lived at Port Jervis in the state of New York. John and Arthur Laughlin, my two brothers, went from New York to Missouri Bend on the Sacramento River in California. After working in New York, I came to John in California.

"I married your grandfather, Reverend King, in California in 1861. He was the son of the old Captain, Richard King, who was running one steamboat on the Missouri and Rio Grande Rivers at that time. He had four sons there. Another one of the boys went west and was lost. Reverend King, your grandfather, was one of Captain Richard King's younger boys. Captain Richard King, your great grandfather, got more boats and ran them on the Rio Grande. He acquired Spanish Land Grants and made the Famous King Ranch of Texas out of them. I told your father, Grovernor Comstock King, about his grandfather, Captain Richard King's marriage to Henrietta Chamberlain.

"Reverend King, your grandfather, was a young minister in the Presbyterian Church and affiliated with the Baptist group that was initiated in and held their meetings in the Presbyterian Church, under the leadership of Rev. R. E. Barnes.

"The Presbyterian Church, where he was minister, burned; Mary's Chapel was built in its place. Rev. King died with pneumonia the year your father was born, 1863. I buried him beside his church in Cacheville, or Yolo cemetery, near Woodland, California.

"After your grandfather died with pneumonia, I bought buckskins from the Indians and made gloves. I tied Grovy to the bedpost with a strap while I was sewing. The strap was long enough so that he could go to sleep on the bed but he never did, he always slept under the bed.

"I married Thomas Jackson Adams, a school chum of Rev. King's and we lived in Cacheville until we moved to Yoncalla, Oregon. At Yoncalla, we lived on Red Hill somewhere near the top. Link and Jimmie Adams walked down to school through the woods. Link would hide in the woods and wait for Jimmie to come from school and then they would both come home.

"Grovernor, your father, was eight years old, and he had a pet colt that he was raising on the bottle. The colt had gone out to pasture so Grovy went to find it; he saw it near a big tree in the meadow. When he got to where it was standing, he saw it jump and look up in the tree where a panther lay on a big branch ready to pounce on them. He ran and jumped on the colt's back and locked his arms around its neck. The terror-stricken colt lunged through the deep grass with Grovy sliding off one side or the other with every jump.

"After Grovy's narrow escape, we moved to Amity, Oregon, and also lived awhile at Sherwood before crossing the river at Penawawa, Washington. Grovy was seventeen then and he stayed with the Finchers. We continued on until we reached the Felch Grove among the greening hills in the hush of twilight. The air was spiced with the incense of the heavy topped evergreens.

"We moved into the tiny house among the trees, and planted the pumpkins—seeds we had brought from Oregon. The children racked up the buffalo chips from the flat for fuel and warmth during the cold and wintry blasts ahead.

"In the spring Thomas Jackson Adams, your step-grandfather, traded a cow for the first quarter of our land here at Pullman. We came to the Four Mile in 1881 and the town of Pullman was founded in 1882. We were very happy when the Washington State College was established in 1891 so Cora and Albert could attend."

We children always begged grandmother to tell us more about our grandfather, Reverend King of Woodland, California. But she always seemed distressed over this deep sorrow in her young life.

After Grandmother Martha King Adams moved to Pullman, my father farmed her land and our quarter at Pullman, besides running the cattle on the Tubbs Spring place and the open range toward Pampa and the Snake River.

We had a house on Grandma's place and one on ours. Papa did all the work with teams and when he did the work on Grandma's land we lived in her house and when he was working on our own land, we moved into the house over by the road. Mattie, my sister, was born in the house on Grandma's place, September 9, 1897.

When she was six days old, mother said, "You may hold the baby."

I was sitting in the rocking chair. Carumba! A feeling of being crushed to near a foot tall froze me to impassitivity.

"For heaven sakes, Grovy! What was that?" she exclaimed.

Something screamed at the side of the house. We listened until it went in front of the house and across the draw. The screams gradually faded away. My father ran to look out the window and found it blown out and splintered. Our neighbor killed the panther.

The next evening, Tommy and I followed the trails across the peaceful green meadow to bring the cows in.

"That cow will stay right on top of the hill until we go and get her," declared Tommy.

So I went up and looked down into the draw, where the sarvis berries in the eyebrow had never been plowed out.

"Tommy, come and see the house," I motioned.

"It is a real house," he said. "Let's go over and look in it!"

A cot, a little bench, a shelf to eat on and a small stove fit into the four by six foot hut.

While I nudged the cows into the corral, Tommy ran to tell Papa.

"Papa, Papa, we found a house over in the draw!" he shouted.

"A claim jumper! I suspect!" cautioned Papa.

"You children go in to your supper and I will investigate."

That night Papa called the neighbors and they all went to the draw and pitched the shack over the fence.

In the fall after he had finished the seeding and was trying to finish the fall plowing, Grovernor King was taken down to his bed with sciatic rheumatism.

Scringing with pain he cried aloud, "I can't be turned to-day, Katie. The pain in my back is excruciating."

She tied his legs together and Grandpa Adams came out from Pullman and helped to turn him.

"You will have to get Grovy out of this cold country," said Grandpa.

Mama nodded her head in agreement, "How can we do it?"

"Turn the horses, machinery and the crop over to Grandma King Adams. She hasn't the money to buy them but she can give you enough to send Grovy to Tuscan Springs in California," suggested Grandpa.

While Papa was at the springs, Mama and we kids took care of Grandfather Fincher's place while Grandpa and Grandma Fincher went to Whitebird, Idaho to visit with Aunt Anna Templeton Chamberlain.

Grandma Mary Fincher couldn't help with the fruit anymore, so she had rented the orchards to Lee Chung, a chinaman from Colfax.

I was going to feed the hen in the coop.

"Don't put your hands in the feed sack without taking it down off the shelf and looking in it," said mother.

I lifted up the coop and a baby rattler dangled from my hand.

"Drop it!" gasped my mother.

When I did, the snake glided away in the grass.

The winds were high, sand was drifting and the white caps were rolling on the river.

Susie Chung came over and was doing the ironing. I went down to the post office in the Simpson Hotel to get the mail and a strange chinaman came to the porch. In his broken English he asked, "When does the steamboat come down the river?"

"It comes before noon," I flung back over my shoulder as I hurriedly shut the door—the wind was cutting my face.

When I came out, he had gone.

Joe Canutt, Sheriff, and Mr. Carter, his deputy, came to mama and asked if we had seen a strange chinaman.

I said, "I saw a chinaman waiting on the porch of the hotel."

They turned their binoculars up the river and sighted him going up through Grandma Fincher's pasture. They followed him up this ravine. They were fresh, and when they got near the top, they called, "Stop! Stop!"

He kept going. Deputy Carter shot at him and the bullet clipped his ear. The chinaman threw his arms up and hollered, "Don't shoot! Don't shoot!"

They handcuffed him and brought him down.

"This highbinder shot another chinaman in the laundry at Colfax during a quarrel," said Sheriff Canutt. "He has disguised himself by dressing in Lee Chung's clothes."

The sheriff brought the highbinder to Colfax for trial and sentence.

My father was walking again after having been treated at the springs, and he stayed with his Aunt Jannie Evers at Chico until he was able to make the trip home. Mama and I met him in Pendleton. The folks lived in Pendleton, Oregon that winter and I came back to Grandma Fincher's.

After pushing my bicycle through the deep dusty road, I reached the Simpson Ferry at Penawawa. I was still wearing the pretty little hat my Aunt Cora Bateman had given me at Waitsburg, Washington.

The days had lost their scorching heat. The air was clear, crisp and cool. The twisted necklets of land that extended out into the river were making rapids above Penawawa and below the Long Hollow. The calmer stretches of water along the five mile bar, where the banks were aflame with the candle red sumacs, were shadowed with a covey of wild ducks going south. The Snake River seemed to be thrust in the crazed volcanic walls to the east. Wrapped in a blanket of content- ment, I sat on a rock and rested. In my hands were so little riches except those given me by God—the water tumbling over the rocks, the burnished red and gold of the blowing trees across the river, the pale yellow of the mullin standing guard over the roadway, and the browning pasture land that had been seared by the heat of a Snake River summer. He was painting the earth with an autumn blush, blazing foliage and flaming hill.

I wondered if the road that we take along life's way would lead onward and upward as this one did today.

Along in the afternoon Mr. Simpson brought me over the river and I rode up through the orchard as fast as my bike would go. There was a wet woody smell in the air as I reached the poplar lined road that went up past Grandma Fincher's house. Red apples carpeted the orchard grass. The trees were bending low with their heavy load.

When I got to Grandma Fincher's, Maida Templeton was there. She had her light Rambler bicycle so we went from Grandma Fincher's up to Grandmother Adams' on the Four Mile.

We stayed all night with our cousin, Nellie Major, near Wilcox. We were going through Wilcox when we met Will Miller.

He asked Maida, "Would you like to go to the May Day dance with me?"

"Would it be all right if my cousin went, too?" she asked.

"Where can I pick you up?" he replied.

"We will be at Ivy Hanna's on our way back to Penawawa."

"I'll see you about eight o'clock in the evening," he said as he drove away.

Going down the prune orchard hill southeast of Colfax, my bicycle got to going too fast for me to brake it with my foot.

"Hang onto your hat," called Maida. "We are going for a ride."

Disaster struck, my front bicycle wheel dropped into a ditch where a culvert had been taken out, and my bicycle went end over end, so did I until I settled in a deluge of dust.

"Did it hurt you, Olive?" Maida asked.

Smiling through my tears, I said, "No! But it sure gave me a devil of a twist."

The road turned right where the trees, that marched from the hill top to the road with their branches intertwined, were laughing in the breeze.

I got my hat in place again and Maida and I went on to Albion to stay all night at Maggie Stover's. Maida stayed with her while I went on to Grandma's on the Four Mile.

On our way back, we stopped at Ivy Hanna's.

The swish of a bustling broom on the porch stopped, a torrent of good will broke into a froth, and their home was filled with gladness when Ivy Hanna called, "Olive and Maida are coming. You children wash your hands and faces."

We had finished eating and were washing the dishes when Maida said, "There is going to be a dance at Wilcox tonight, Ivy. We have been invited to go."

"I don't have anything to wear! I really don't, Ivy," I said. "Unless I could wear my black georgette crepe skirt and my pink silk blouse, that I left at Aunt Anna's."

"Why wouldn't that be all right? You can wear a black velvet ribbon around your neck," said Maida. "I'll wear my new dress that mother just finished with the ruffled yoke and a ribbon in my hair."

Ivy helped us to get our clothes pressed. We washed our hair, styled it in a roll up the back with a puff in front and combed in a switch.

It was a warm day late in May and low clouds, that looked like soap bubbles, crowned the wild flowered hills beneath the vaulted sky. The tall grass flicked by the breeze made a brushing sound. The shadowy line of willows bent in sympathy over the grass, caressing it with the tips of their long green fronds. The trees, heavy with bloom, cast a resinous pungency into the air.

The clip-clop of the steel shod hooves of the horses as they came near made our spirits soar.

"Are you girls ready to go?" he asked affably, a smile curling his lips.

His blue eyes were friendly when he said, "I am Will Miller and I came to take Maida and Olive to the dance, Mrs. Hanna."

He reigned the horses and helped us into the one seated buggy that had a curtained top that buttoned behind the seat. "Fleetfoot" flossed his mane and tugged at the bit. The other horse just winked. He tapped them with his buggy whip and a cascade of dust soon shut us from view.

As evening was merging into night, we began to hear the lilting strains of an old refrain, "The Irish Washer Woman," as Jim Davis drew the bow across the strings up in the Yeoman Hall above the Whitten store at Wilcox. We joined the Grand March and had a wonderful get-together with everyone we knew.

When I danced with Lloyd Simpson, we won a watch for the best waltzers.

Maida and I took the floor. We both danced a lot with Will, and chattered all the way home to Ivy's. We snuck upstairs to bed and ate an early breakfast with Ivy and the family. I went back to Penawawa in a few days and helped Aunt Sadie and Uncle Cota with the rest of their fruit.

Will came down to see me on Sundays for the rest of the summer.

Mattie, my sister, came up to stay with me. She would cry to go with us when we went riding in the buggy, so Will would say, "Yes, Grandma come on. You can go too."

Riding along the road, the first Sunday that she went with us, we heard the raucous call of a sharp-clawed chicken hawk as he measured the distance from post to post. The blue racer that we had cut in two with the buggy wheel lay wriggling in the track. When we came back the hawk had taken his prey!

Mrs. Elza Smith and Elva had moved to Colfax and Uncle Cota had leased her orchard. Nora O'dell, Esther O'dell, Maida and I were packing the fruit for Uncle Cota. Faye Templeton and Gene Jones were the foremen during the fruit harvest on the Elza Smith place.

From folding ladders the pickers took the fruit from the tree and put it into a basket. The baskets were hauled to the newly constructed packing house on a fruit cart drawn by one horse. The picking crew brought ten or twelve baskets at a time to the packing house. The pickers carried the fruit in and set it on the floor in the middle of the packing shed. Maida and I picked up a basket and set it on the packing bench at our own station. A helper carried the box away, after it was packed, to a man behind us who finished the box by putting on the lid and stamping the name of the grower on it. This man set the boxes in the end of the packing house. From the packing house they hauled them away in a fruit cart to the boat landing where the steamboats came in and dropped their gang planks, up beyond the mouth of the Penawawa Creek.

Each grower stacked his boxes in a separate pile. When the steamboat came in, the riverman came down the plank with a loader and took the boxes, a few at a time, keeping Mr. Cota's fruit separate from the rest, although it was stamped with his name.

I explained to Maida, "Pack the peach by picking up the wrapping paper in the left hand, the peach in the right. Place the peach in the paper, blossom end down, and twist the paper to close. Then put seven peaches in the first row and five in the next. Start the next layer with five wrapped peaches and then seven. We will alternate the layers until the box is filled and weighs about twenty pounds. The box man will cleat on the far end of the top and nest the fruit down before cleating it to close.

The fruit crew was dusty and tired after a day's work in the boiling sun so we all got together and went swimming, which we thought was refreshing for our minds, bodies and souls. Archie Derbin, Uncle Cota's cousin, went in the crowd to see that we didn't get in too deep.

"This river has a narrow, deep channel in the middle and the undertow is very strong where the water sweeps out over the wide ledges and sucks back into the main channel," he told us. "Go out until you feel the undertow and then come back."

The cool water was lapping the sun kissed sands.

"Leon, you have to swim today!" declared Uncle Cota.

"I can't swim, father," pleaded Leon.

Uncle Cota in desperation grabbed him and threw him into the shallow water. Leon panicked, stiffened and began to sink and drift.

"Help me, Archie! For God sakes help me! He is going down," called his father.

Archie swam toward him from up river and Uncle Cota went down deep and brought him up. Together they got him to shore.

Faye Templeton had taken time away from his seigning

grounds above the ferry landing at the end of Main Street to work in the fruit, so after we dressed we went up where his crew of three men were getting ready to let out the seign.

They put the seign in the boat and fastened one end along the bank. Then the men who were doing the rowing circled out in the river and rowed out the full length of the seign. Two men rowed and one man sat in the back of the boat and let out the seign. Then they "rowed in" and pulled in the upper end of the seign, which had fifteen pink salmon (weighing fifteen to twenty pounds each) in it. They were struggling to free themselves of the net and one did cut it and get away. The men flipped the rest of the salmon into the trap in the front of the boat and "tied up" for the night. Purse seigns were not prohibited on the river until 1917.

On the way home Maida asked, "What are you going to do after harvest?"

"I'm going up to the folks. They live in a little house on the knoll above the Palouse River where Potlatch is soon to be built," I explained.

By the time I got home, after finishing the fruit harvest, Papa was clearing the eighty acres, that we intended to buy, with the team. He was encouraged by an old man who lived in the flat.

"They are planning to build a sawmill on this eighty acres of stump land, Mr. King!" he told my father.

The Potlatch Lumber Company purchased the land, built the sawmill and the town began to grow.

Because my folks didn't want me to get married, I moved with them to Walla Walla, renewed my eighth grade certificate and went into nurses training in the Dr. Crop Hospital.

There were eighteen nurses in this hospital owned by Dr. Crop, a medium sized man with blue eyes and brown hair.

It was early in the afternoon. Mrs. Fowler, my roommate, and I were studying for a test in anatomy.

"The building! It's burning!" echoed down the hall.

The hospital supervisor was giving orders. As she came to our door she said, "Miss King and Mrs. Fowler, take the babies and children out."

When we got the children to the lawn from the first floor nursery, we could hear the horse-drawn fire engine coming.

"R-R-R-ooooooo ble! R-R-R-ooooooo ble!"

Rumbling wheels drowned out our voices. The firemen wearing coats, boots and helmets attached the pumper engine to the hydrant. Water from the hydrant was pumped through the hose and forced high up and out into the burning building.

Some of the patients were not confined to their beds and had gotten up for the afternoon so they walked out, but the operative patients had to be carried by the nurses, orderlies and firemen.

The fire chief shouted orders, "Firemen one and two take blankets and help carry out the patients! Firemen three and four go up with the ladders and cut holes in the roof with your axes to let out the gas! Five and six shoot water into the upper story! Seven and eight take a hose inside the building and chop the doors through to let out the smoke!"

The firemen stopped the fire and kept it from spreading. They came back to the fire engine, rolled up their hose and, after hanging up their ladders on each side of the truck, drove away. The clanging of the bell was a welcome sound, the fire was out.

One elderly patient, who was very ill, had passed away, and one of the tiny babies died. The other patients were given individual care.

I was assigned to St. Vincent's Hospital in Portland for the completion of my nurses training. My mother was stepping off a foot bridge and grazed the step of the approach, breaking her ankle bone, so I stayed home and took care of her.

I went to work in the alteration department of the Fair Store before going into the suit department of Motter Wheelers.

I had been in the store about a year, when Mr. Cooper, the manager, announced, "I'm putting the laces in your department, Wiolet!" I knew that the laces wouldn't sell so I walked out the front door. Mr. Cooper went out the side door and met me on the street.

"Now, Wiolet, you don't have to sell the lace! You can model the suits and hats," he said apologetically.

And I did. I wore one of the elegant roll brimmed hats home for lunch, and stopped at the Britton Photographer's Gallery on North Main. I sat in the chairs outside the shop and had my picture taken. Two-year-old Cecil Britton, a baby with yellow curly hair, blue eyes, big arched wide brows and ruddy complexion was playing on the street making up with all the people who passed.

One day while at work, I saw the Brittons pull up to the curb in front of the store. Mrs. Britton's face was as pale as her dress. Mr. Britton boosted her out of the buggy and they seemed to be telling Mr. Sanderson something. I went over near the door where I could hear what they were saying.

"After setting up camp in the Blue Mountains where we were planning to spend the week-end," Mrs. Britton said, "I spread down a blanket in a little clearing on the edge of the woods and placed the baby on the blanket. I wanted to rest before starting to cook our dinner so I lay down beside the boy. I was listening to the lacey fronds of the cedars making a brushing sound like the wings of the wind. I watched the clouds that looked like white sheep on a blue hill until I fell asleep.

"When I woke up two-year-old Cecil was gone. My heart speeded up, beads of perspiration stood out on my forehead, my mouth was dry and I felt faint. Mr. Britton dropped the wood he was carrying for the fire and came running.

"Someone has taken our baby, Ben!" I screamed. "Why did you leave us so long?

"With fear and trembling and with dismay, we kept going toward the A tent by the crackling fire. He pleaded with me to rest while he searched the campgrounds."

"Sight of his cap beside the stream in the wood intensified my fear. After searching along the stream, I hastened back to the camp, harnessed the horses, and as soon as we could load our camping equipment we raced through the low underbrush until we reached the main road," prompted Mr. Britton.

"You left for the camp in the early afternoon?" questioned Mr. Sanderson, the policeman, who had been walking his beat past the store.

Mr. Sanderson rode away with the Brittons.

When I came home that night, Mama had heard from the Sanderson's, who were our next door neighbors, that "Cecil Britton was lost."

Despite many days of searching by all of the people who had transportation, Cecil Britton was never found.

Tommy, my brother, went up to Penawawa to work for Charlie Haines. He and Mr. Haines were pitching hay when they heard a team coming down the road. He and Tommy went right down to the road. The horses had been running a long ways. Tommy hit one of the horses across the nose to stop him and he dropped dead. There were two men in the buggy, Dr. Ferguson and Sheriff Wineburg. Both of them were big fat men and they were bouncing from one side of the buggy to the other. Their faces were white with fright. They were grieved about their horse but glad to get out. They were relieved that someone could stop them some way. Dr. Ferguson reprimanded Sheriff Wineburg saying, "Why did you let them get started to running?"

"They pulled the reins out of my hands," Mr. Wineburg retorted.

The men stayed at Charlie Haines' until a rig came from Colfax to pick them up. Tommy and Charlie buried the horse.

When I was twenty-three, in 1908, I came back to Penawawa to work in the fruit on the George Pierce place. Grandfather Emsley Fincher had received a good price from the Camas Prairie Railroad for the crossing of his land by the railroad that was started in 1906. It followed the buffalo trails along the river grades. Completed in 1908, by 1909 the Union Pacific began to use the Northern Pacific branches extending eastward and south eastward from Lewiston under a 999 year lease for operating convenience. These jointly used lines were called the Camas Prairie Railroads, but their earnings and expenses were apportioned to the two owning railroad systems.

At first the railroad companies were not going to give Grandfather Emsley Fincher what he wanted for the land. So he set up a tent out in the area where they had to go through and lived in it. While he went to Colfax to sit in on the lawsuit with the railroad officials, Grandmother Mary went down and lived in the tent until Grandfather Emsley came home with his quoted price.

Gus Miller, Will's father, decided to move to Colfax and rent his ranch to Will and Mack, his brother. Will and I decided to get married and I would cook for them while they did the farming.

I told George Pierce, "I'm going to get married so I will not be able to help with your fruit harvest."

He became angry as he said, "Why didn't you tell me?"

"We didn't know what Father Miller was planning to do," I replied.

Then he laughed, and said, "Someone can take your station."

The Finchers

When the wind has carved an eyebrow
　　On the north side of the hill,
And the rain soft and gentle
　　Carries loess into the rills.
We may see a road that leads
　　Across the ledge and fill,
Past the Fincher house
　　Part of which stands still.
Over in the meadows
　　Where their children loved to play,
In their earthy beds they sleep
　　For God has called them all away.

Chapter IV

OVER IN THE MILLER MEADOWS

Augustus Miller drew rein at the falls in the Spokane River and made ready to bed down for the night at the edge of the boulder-filled canyon, green with pine trees.[4] Wearily flinging off his chaps he gulped the swift flowing water of the stream from where he sprawled across the rocks. On the high ledges the coyotes were yelping, and he listened to the echoing of their calls. As blue curling smoke from the burning fire mingled with the purple deep of night, the smell of the melting pine pitch hovered over the flame. Snuggled in his saddle blankets and with his head nestled in his saddle, he fell asleep beside the fire.

The next morning a faint wind from the prairie flattened the brim of his hat, as he mounted his cayuse and started south toward a prairie horizon where acre upon acre of bunch-grass rustled, waiting. The wind was moving clouds that cast shadows on the GRASS THAT WAS GOLD.

The sun, devoid of heat and brilliance, was dropping low over the Palouse Hills before Augustus stationed himself on the towering rocks. He caught a glimpse of a pine covered hill and the far reaching peaceful countryside, where the overturned yellowish-brown loess met some thinning stubble.

---

4 By 1878 the town of Spokane had one store, a small flour mill, a saw mill, a blacksmith shop and nine families lived there. K. M. Cowley bridge was fifteen miles up the river. Lapwai bridge was twenty miles down the river. Winters were six months long with twenty degrees below zero weather. The Northern Pacific Railroad was expecting to build in the area.

He had pursued the narrow trail aloft the south side of the bluff, through a cluster of young birch trees, across the horizontal bench of patient grass—intermingled with blotches of purple lupine and touches of yarrow—to the rocky ledge, where the many massive flows of basalt, that underlie the deep mantel of wind-deposited soil and volcanic ash, protrude.

As he ran a caressing hand down the neck of his horse, the horse turned his head and looked into the face of Gus Miller, whose eyes darkened with a brooding sadness. A strange longing filled his heart as he scrutinized the knolls shaped by the southwest winds into dunes sloping gently to the northeast. Cattle were bawling below him on the grassy uplands. The fending of the heifers through the brush along the North Palouse made a cracking sound. The calls of the mothers for their young echoed under the bluff and lingered after the yearlings were far up the slopes.

Gus' keen blue eyes softened and darkened as he marveled at the swirling brown, turgid South Palouse River slowed at its confluence by the rising heave of water from the North Palouse. From here the Palouse River turns southwest to whittle from the rock the intricate drainage pattern that parallels that of the Snake River and flows into it—a breathless thrill for a man cultivating a dream.

A wavy line of elongated town flanked the two branches of the Palouse River. Low bleached, board and baton houses were strung along their tortuous banks. Serving the people of Colfax were Warren Belcher's drygoods store, D. Wolford and Joseph Davenport's general merchandise store, J. M. Nosler's hotel, J. C. Davenport's lumber mill and flouring mill, two churches and a school.

Gus continued on to the south until he reached the homestead of his brother, Henry Miller, who took possession of his land over in the Miller meadows on the Penawawa Creek in 1875. In 1876, the first wheat was shipped from Whit-

man County at the Almota dock, and fifteen wagons, four
threshers, three sulky plows, three reapers and three headers
were brought on the steamer's return trip from Portland,
Oregon.

Gus' mother, Mary Salina Hartzig Miller, and his brother,
Guilford Miller, lived in the lower meadow.

"Why don't you bring Lila and the family out west?" asked
Guilford. "They are beginning to grow wheat on the flat
and there is open range for cattle. As much as ten thousand bushels of wheat at eight dollars per ton freight have
gone out from Almota."

"Albert is riding range this year on Baldy," said his mother.
"They will soon be rounding up and branding. Wouldn't you
like to help with the round-up this year?"

"I would but I promised Lila to be back by the time the
work starts in the woods," he informed her.

Leaving Dushore, Pennsylvania in the fall of 1884, he
brought his wife, Delilah Ann Weaver Miller and their four
boys—Henry, 12, John, 10, Will, 8, and Ellery, 6—to Colfax
on the Northern Pacific Railroad. The Northern Pacific not
only brought many settlers from the eastern United States and
Europe into the county, but it also marketed wheat and other
grains.

The homes on the north flat that resembled small farms
were surrounded with wooden fences to enclose a stable for
the driving team and shelter for chickens, a cow or other
animals.

The clang of iron shoes on the brick streets broke the silence
as the Millers rode down toward the north flat.

When they got to the house they had rented on the flat, Gus
asked cautiously, "Lila, I think we will be comfortable here,
don't you?"

"Of, course!" she said as she swallowed hard. "We will only
be here a year!"

Most of the year had passed when two-month-old Royal was strickened with typhoid fever and died.

"Will and John are very sick," their mother told her neighbors. "All I can give them to eat is brown gravy. I have to boil the water that we drink and all of our dishes."

After days of delirium and high fever her children began to improve. Their Grandmother Mary Miller helped to care for them until they recovered.

"We have had walking typhoid, mother," said Gus. "We must find a better place to rear our family."

So they purchased the Henry Miller homestead for $1,200 and moved out there before it was winter.

In the spring, Grandmother Miller's cows came up the meadow to the fence between the two farms and the boys set the dogs on them. Dogging the cows made them hold back their milk.

"Henry, John, Will and Ellery! Your grandmother is coming up the flat," called their mother. "Have you been chasing the cows again?"

Henry, John, Will and Ellery were nowhere to be seen. They had been looking for their grandmother long before she came in sight of the house.

"Here she comes," said Henry. "Let's go over the hill and hide."

"You lead the way and we will follow you," said John.

"Will, you help Ellery."

Flying legs and feet beat a path over the hill and down into the draw. Hunkered against the fence in the tall grass they felt safe with their hounds, "You Know" and "I Know."

"Ephriam Wicks has some horses that need breaking and taming. Maybe he would let us ride them," said John.

"Naw," said Henry. "You're too little."

It was several years before Will and John helped break horses for Mr. Wicks and got the loan of them for doing their farm work. John and Will loved their horses from the time they lassoed and staked the first cayuse that ran to the end of the rope and broke away.

"They are opening a college at Pullman in the fall and I want you boys to go," said their mother. "Henry will go this year and John next."

"Where will we live?" asked Henry.

"We will rent a house and you can batch."

Will, a fine, young man, had insight and the courage to carry it out.

"I'll take up the food, mother," he said, and he did.

In winter he hitched two horses to the four-runner bobsled and filled the bed with hay. In the hay he packed and covered the food—meat, potatoes, butter, eggs and fruit—with lap robes.

He put on his fur hat, big gloves with fur cuffs, and an ankle-length fur overcoat that had three black buttons up the front, that were just black bars with a snap elastic hook. The coat had a wide collar that could be turned up and wide turn-back cuffs. When he didn't wear four buckle galoshes, he wrapped his feet with gunny sacks. He had a way of folding the cut open sacks so that they were a triangle. He brought the sides across the top leaving them high at the back and the two sides, crossing them over the corner that had been brought up over the toe, and tying them on top of the foot.

"Man it was cold!" Will told his mother. "So I put the horses in the livery stable and stayed all night with Henry."

When spring came Father Miller got about eight hives of bees and put them under the box elder trees in front of the house.

"It is June, Lila," he said. "Haven't you heard the drowsy humming of the bees? I'm going to take the honey out of the hives."

"Your bee mask is in the smoke house," she said, "and your gloves are here in the drawer."

Father put on the wire mask covered with netting and tied it around his neck. He put on his gloves and took the pans and knives.

"Our honey has the taste of clover," he told Henry. "It must be the best honey in the world."

"It is pure honey," said Henry. "The bees only use one kind of nectar and they have been working in our red and white clover field."

"Did you know that the working bee dies in flight struggling to get back to the hive with her load?" asked Henry.

"Do you know how they make the nectar into honey, Henry?" asked Father.

"In the hive the field bees pump out the little cargo of nectar from their crops in their mouths into the mouths of the young stay-at-home bees. The stay-at-home bees thrust their tongues in and out to evaporate the water from the nectar and add enzymes that convert the sugars into levulose and dextrose," explained Henry.

"How do they make the combs?"

"The wax on the honey comb comes from the bee's own glands. When he has filled a cell with honey, he closes it with wax and the enzymes continue to grow until the 'green honey' becomes 'ripe honey'."

"How do they pollinate the crops?"

"The bodies of the bees fit into some flower forms and they use the pollen and nectar for pollination. Mother uses it to sweeten and preserve foods because bacteria can't live in the concentrated sugar more than an hour and you children have good teeth. It keeps the calcium in the body and builds good bones as well as solid teeth."

"There is going to be a picnic at the Johnson Grove," interrupted Ellery. "Mother wants to go."

"Tell her to get ready," said Gus.

It was the custom to wear a most beautiful white apron to the community picnics at Dushore, Pennsylvania so Delilah Ann Weaver Miller starched a lovely apron and wore it to the grove.

One of the young people who didn't know about this custom said, "apron!" and his friends joined in a big guffaw. This hurt Lila Miller's feelings, so she didn't take the boys so often to these annual picnics. They entertained themselves at home.

"Let's play mumble peg," said Phil.

"I'll draw a circle around the peg with this stick, and no one is to go inside the circle.

"We will count down for turns," said Roy. "Everybody kneel down outside the circle."

"Henry is first," said John.

He flipped his knife but stayed on the ground. The boy that was second lost control of his knife and it cut through Henry's eyeball.

"Come, quick! Mother! Henry is hurt!" shouted Will.

His mother washed and dressed his eye with cotton and tape and they started for town, thirteen miles with the team. Dr. Blalock was up from Walla Walla and he treated Henry's eye until it healed.

After Henry attended the Washington State College at Pullman for seven years, he went to Washington, D. C. with Dr. Spillman and worked in the Agricultural Department for forty years.

A major contribution was made by W. S. Spillman, who began studies on wheat hybrids in 1890 at the Washington State University Experiment Station at Pullman. Continued work at the station beginning in 1907 has developed such important varieties of wheat as Elmer, Brevor, and Gaines No. 1 and No. 2, which have been planted on the farms in Whitman County, first as seed wheat and then for commercial use.

John finished in accounting and became the Clerk of Whitman County. Will stayed with the Mathew Johnson family and attended the Old English College at Colfax, where he was outstanding in mental arithmetic.

One day when he and John were out to the ranch, they were sitting against the fence—entwined with green vines and weeds—that rambled over the hill and across the field. The gray squirrels were playing on the mounds that encircled every post.

"How would you like to get rich, John?" Will asked.

"What would you do?" John asked interestedly.

"Do big farming!" suggested Will.

"We could get rich if we had enough land!" Will thought.

"How will we get it? How?"

"Well, we could buy some and lease the rest!"

"Guilford may want to sell someday! Maybe we could get that lease and the one on Cornwall's and on Patterson's land."

They were seized by a swift and stunning ambition and had the foresight and physical strength to carry it out. Drawing energy and inspiration from their homes, churches and neighbors with whom they conversed in silence they grew in the soil together.

They formed the Miller Bros. and paid for the land now contained in the three Miller ranches with the help of their brother Ellery, who was stricken with paralysis in his right arm when he was attending the Business College in Spokane. He was laying carpet in the evenings to help pay for his school supplies and the constant use of his arm developed a condition that gradually improved until he could use his arm again. But he did not return to the school. He went into partnership with his brothers.

"Auntie Gus had a wonderful family," as recalled by a neighbor, Edrie Adams.

They attended church at Onecho, where the Methodist

Church was organized in the late seventies. M. S. Anderson was named to be the first preacher or regular charge north of the Snake River. He organized the churches of Onecho and Colfax. Will Miller married Olive Pearl King at Colfax, June 21, 1908 at the Methodist Parsonage, and Ellery Miller married Mattie Matilda King, December 25, 1914, in the Methodist Church at Colfax. The King girls were great grand-daughters of Captain Richard King of Kingsville, Texas.

Reverend M. S. Anderson served for some time as the circuit rider pastor. He later came back and served the church again.

The group of hardy Christians worshipped together until about 1889, when more of the Mennonites arrived, headed by the Aeschlimans and the Rubins. The cathedral, Aeschliman Von Longnau, was built in honor of the Aeschliman family in Berne, Switzerland, which was their original homeland. Delilah Ann Weaver Miller's father, Barnhardt Weaver, was a descendant of a very old French-Swiss and Mennonite family. This new group was very welcome to the pioneer Methodists as they were good singers and the natives were not noted for that art.

They worshipped together several years in the old schoolhouse. When it was decided to build the church, it was first a toss-up whether the building should belong to the Methodists or the Mennonites, there being the same number of each.

After due consideration the Methodist folks said to the Mennonites, "You men are good carpenters, you build the church and we will help."

The land was deeded by J. J. Tompkins. Thus, the problem was settled and they worshipped together for sixty years, proving that people who do not agree on all doctrinal points can worship the same God in the same house and be happy about it.

Because Lila Miller preferred her mother's church to that

of her father's faith, she baptized Henry, John, Will and Ellery Miller when they were each one year old in their grandmother's church, the Thrasher Church (Drescher) of Dushore, Pennsylvania. Land for the Zion Lutheran Church and cemetery was given by their Great Grandfather, George Thrasher, born 1774 at Reading, Pennsylvania.

The four Miller boys attended the church, built on Tompkins' land, with children from the families of Tompkins, Hickman, Johnsons, Odells, Wamires and Aeschlimans.

When they entered the school Lou Aeschliman was in the first grade. The Miller boys spoke Pennsylvania Dutch dialect and everyone laughed when they recited. The only words that Will remembered were, "Buva Vinga Veita," meaning "the boys are teasing again."

His first day in school he held up his hand to be excused and the teacher said, "Yes, if it is necessary." When he got home he asked his mother, "Mother, what does 'GENARY' mean?" This probably explains why he got to wear his Sunday suit to school the next day.

Lila Miller had many good neighbors. She walked almost every week to Anna Templeton's, usually with something for her, which was often cuttings that she had started for Anna. Anna came and helped her with some tasks like wall-papering when mother Miller didn't know how to start in the middle and work out to the ends.

After Will and I were married, mother Miller and I cooked for the heading crew—Uncle Guilford Miller, Gene Weaver, Carlton Saxon, John Hayes, Father Augustus Miller and my husband.

I loved to smell the tantalizing aroma of the fresh, dry hay overflowing the mows of the barn, to hear the pigeons cooing in the gable, to see fields of ripe golden wheat and to trudge through the deep dust of the winding, ragged, steep and lonely road to the old place. The back road with its gooseberry bushes and elder tree curled around my heart.

We got up at three o'clock in the morning. Mother took the coal oil lamp from the wall bracket and held the lighted match to it. While the clock, on the shelf over the table, ticked away the hour, we put breakfast on the table by four.

"Olive, will you fill the coffee pot and put in twelve tablespoons of coffee?" she asked quietly. "I'll chop the potatoes and butter them so they can go into the oven. Now, while I mix the soda biscuits, you can fry the bacon and eggs."

The bubbling tea kettle hissed and filled the room with a homey cheer. I put the rolled oats in the boiling water on the back of the stove.

The quick bark of Cool, the collie, told us that the men were coming from the barn.[5] Hands that worked earnestly the whole day through turned down the lanterns and set them on the porch.

We could hear the sloshing water and the creaking handle of the pump. They "washed up" in the basins that set on the bench by the pump outside the kitchen door. Most of the men drank from the spilly dipper before coming in. While they ate their breakfast, they planned their work for the day.

"Guilford, Gene and Carlton, take your four horse header-box teams ahead and I will follow you with my eight horse header team," said Will.

Will was a tall, good-looking, young man who could go ahead and get things done. He had the strength to reap the grain nurtured by the melting snows of winter, the heat of summer sun and the gentle rains that fall on the wind swept

---

5 Cool laid around the house until Father Miller came for the milk buckets. Then he would go right out and get the cows and bring them to the barn for milking. Mother Miller made butter with a dasher churn and wooden butter molds. Father took ten pounds of butter and a double crate of eggs to town and sold them every week.

Palouse Hills. The Palouse Hills, forcing up the southwesterly winds from the ocean cause them to yield twelve to twenty inches of rain a year. The rainfall increases from twelve inches on the western side of the county to twenty-four inches on the Idaho border. The increase in organic content of the soil is encouraged by the heavier rainfall and the cold nights.

"We will cut with the header. The drapper will carry the wheat into the two nets in your header boxes. When you get to the derrick, the team will pull one net at a time from the header box, trip and drop it over the stack. When Nordyke gets the threshing outfit set up, we will unload right onto the derrick table and the hoe downs will feed the wheat into the separator," advised Will.

"Claude Wilkerson is the best derrick man we ever had work for us. Art Hibler is his roustabout and he brought some trappings over yesterday so we haven't any time to lose. John can drive the derrick and father will stack."

After the men had hit for the field, mother opened the door of the kitchen stove and sparks flew out the lower draft as she filled the wood over the grate. The wood smoke smelled sweet.

"I'll knead the dough, shape the loaves and put them in pans to raise, if you will bring in cherries and apples from the orchard for the pies, Olive," offered mother.

I went to the orchard through the fence where it was low and easy to get through. The long grass slipping under my feet caused me to discover a quail's nest hidden behind a post in the weedy fence row. The little mother's black eyes glinted at me as I scrambled up the bank.

The trees were heavy ladened with Bings, Royal Anns and Tartans. The spice of the yellow harvest apples, nestled in the matted grass, came from along the hill. The wind was blowing free and I filled my lungs with the fruity scented air. The whirr of a Chinese pheasant's wings rent the silence, and brown squirrels scurried to their mounds, straightened, cheeped and dropped out of sight.

I picked the ripest of the luscious cherries from the leafy boughs of the trees and the firmest of the apples, that were windfalls, from the ground.

"Come and see the quail's nest, mother!" I called as I climbed back through the fence.

"We won't let her know we saw her," she said. "This will be our secret."

We pitted the cherries and quartered and cored the apples. Then mother baked a cake for the evening meal while I cut the lard into the flour, added salt and hot water for my pie crust, rolled it out to about a quarter of an inch thick and pressed it over my four pie tins. I put in the cooked and sweetened fruit and covered them with a perforated crust and fluted the edges together with my thumb and finger. They were browned by the time the cake was baked so we put the roast in the oven by nine o'clock, and mixed the gravy after the meat was done.

From the garden, we brought potatoes and carrots, cleaned, peeled and put them on the stove about eleven.

Cottage cheese, made by putting clabber milk on the back of the stove and cooking, draining and mixing it with salt, pepper and sour cream dressing, was a part of the meal along with applesauce.

When we didn't have a roast, we would kill four chickens by wringing their necks off, scalding them in a pail of boiling water, picking, singeing them with a burning newspaper, washing and putting them in cold water to bleach. After cutting them across the breast, we drew them and cut them up.

By twelve o'clock the kitchen was steeped with the smell of freshly baked homemade bread, pies, browned beef and the sweet aroma from the coffee grinder—the table was neatly spread.

They had only been out about an hour in the afternoon when Claude Wilkerson rode up to the front gate and dropped his reins over the post.

Mother went out to see what he wanted thinking that he had probably come in to fill the water canteens.

"Mrs. Miller, can you bind up my hand?" he said. "The derrick driver didn't listen for my call and started too soon. I caught my hand in the pulley."

"I have some turpentine! Can you stand it if I pour it full of turpentine!" she taunted.

Claude, a very large strong man, said, "Sure pour away."

We pressed his fingers flat, bound the hand with clean white muslin and he went back and worked the rest of the afternoon.

Father Miller worked in his blacksmith's shop keeping all the machinery running and the horses shod. He built a very large bellows to make the forgefire glow.

"Work the bellows until the horseshoes are white hot!" he told Ellery. "We will use number two shoes for Snip. I'll hold the horse's leg between my knees and shape the shoes to fit each of his feet with the tongs. Hold the bucket of water so I can drop each one of the shoes in the pail to cool.

"Now we will drive the flat nails up through the bottom of the shoe so that they go out through the side of the hoof without touching the frog in the horse's foot. Then we will cut off any nails that are too long and clench them before we rasp the hoof down smooth to the shoe." An acrid smell soon filled the shop.

"We will need the water left in the pail for the grindstone," continued Father. "After you pour it on and while you are turning the wooden handle, I'll sharpen the sickle for the mower." Sparks flew from the wheel.

Ellery turned and turned, "I'm getting tired, Father. It's getting warm in this shop."

When the straw had built a stack and the golden grain

stopped flowing into the sack, the harvest was over. This was the first year the Miller boys did not do heading on the outside.

Will and John began hauling the tiered piles of sacks in wagons to Mockanema. While Boone Freeman fed the horses and cattle, Guy McFadden did some of the fall plowing. Gene Weaver helped with all of the fall work and then stayed through the winter and fed cattle.

As soon as the air began to get nippy we butchered. The neighbors brought their hogs to our kill. The wives of the men who brought hogs helped to get the dinner for the men doing the butchering.

We fattened more hogs than we needed for our own use and sold them to the college at Pullman. Eight or ten men butchered together. They ran the hogs into a pen, shot them in the head, put them through the scalding vat and rolled them out with ropes onto the scraping bench. Two men took the scrapers in their hands, a flat cup with a handle, and scraped the hair off the hog. By cutting through the tendons on the back of the leg and running a gamble stick through the slits, each hog could be hung on the gamble stick over the scaffold. After scrubbing the hog and making the hide white, they drew them by cutting the hog through the belly and dropping the insides into a tub. They saved the heart, liver and tongue and buried the waste in a pit.

Trimmings from the hams, shoulders and side pieces were saved for sausage. The hams, shoulders and bacon slabs were put on a big table and dry salted by putting a layer of meat, of dry salt and then of meat. (The other men took their meat home and cut it up.)

Each piece of ham, shoulder and bacon slabs was hung by a string in the smokehouse. Poles and wires held the pieces of meat apart. A fire was built in an old stove with the lids off and just enough pipe to make it draw. After the fire had been kept burning for several days and the meat was thoroughly cured, a brown paper bag was drawn over each piece and tied at the top to keep it clean until it was used.

Putting the trimmings from the meat into a sausage grinder, running them into a tub and working the seasoning in with our hands, we pressed the ground sausage into the stuffer, which filled it into the sheep casings. The casings, which had been turned wrong side out and cleaned, were bought at the butcher shop. We coiled the sausage into half gallon jars and sealed it. When we heated the jars for sealing, the lard formed on the top of the jar and gave added protection.

For sealing the pig feet we had scraped and packed in jars, we filled the jar with a pickling solution.

After sawing the meaty parts of the heads lengthwise and cooking them, we took the meat off for the making of head-cheese.

After we rendered the lard from fifteen heavy, fat hogs in a large black iron kettle, we poured it into five gallon tin cans and sold it at the grocery store.

Cracklings left from the lard rendering we used for making soap.

"I'll build a fire under the kettle that is hanging on the iron bar over the pit," offered Will.

"I'll need some help mixing the formula of cracklings and lye," I assured him.

"How long does it have to cook?" asked Thelma.

"Five hours and then we let it cool," I estimated.

"Can I see the soap, mother?"

"No, not until the soap collects on the top of the kettle and father cuts it into bars. You can help put it out on the planks to drain and dry."

I cooked for the men who were building John's house. It took a long time to build it. Ellery helped me cook for the crew. He took off his coat and came into the kitchen to cook. He was a good one, too. John wanted to put his house up where the first old Miller house stood along the road toward Wilcox, where the old road went over the hill and down into the draw. Ellery asked him what he was going to do the day he started to survey the lot for the house. John went ahead and surveyed anyway.

After father and mother moved into the Warmuth house in Colfax, Will and John were shipping their hogs out on the railroad from Colfax. They got up at three o'clock in the morning and loaded the hogs. Will didn't wake me up when he left the house, so when the men got the hogs loaded and came to the house for their breakfast they didn't have any; however, despite the delay the stock went out on the railroad to Spokane that day.

After they formed the partnership, the three men did their own plowing.

The corn shocks had a heavy dew on them early in the morning before we moved down to the lower place in 1913. After thoroughly cleaning the house, we moved down our furniture, clothes and fruit.

Our four-year-old daughter, Thelma, enjoyed riding from one house to the other. Our second child, Willma, came in the following year, September 28, 1914.

Chapter V

RUNNING WATER

Will, a good teamster, was on the ladder that extended out over the horses and ran both legs through it on the overturn. Orin Martin, the sack sewer, got up with his sack needle in his mouth. Lute Templeton, the separator tender, went off over the high side and came down to help Will get loose from the ladder. He was still yelling, "Whoa!" when Lute got to him.

"The way you held onto that umbrella is sure something!" urged Lute.

"We rolled her! That's something sure!" Will snapped impatiently.

Pulling over a knoll, the team swung down the hill and tipped over the old Holt Combine, a ground power that didn't level. The twenty-four head of horses ripped the harness loose from the hitches, and together with Rocks and two other leaders, ran through the flat to the corral gate.

"We'll never catch them now, Will!" Martin called in panic.

"I couldn't reach the leaders with the air gun!" Will explained nervously. "We'll turn them in and unharness them and then we'll mend all of the broken straps," he said in a stern voice.

Will, John and Lute went out and picked up the doubletrees, singletrees and butt chains. They replaced all the disjointed parts, and "rigged them out."

103

They erected the machine the second day, set up and cut in the afternoon.[6]

Orin, the sack sewer, looped the twine around his hand and tied the ear on the left. He sewed the hemmed edges by running the flat needle—threaded with the twine—through and looping back, and then he tied the ear on the right. He filled the chute with five sacks and dumped them in the same place each time around the hill.

The wheat haulers were picking up the sacks out of the row of dumps from the draws to the top of the hills and loading them onto the wagons.

"Mother! Mother!" I could hear Thelma, my daughter, calling, but I couldn't see her.

I ran to the orchard and took her out of the crotch of the cherry tree where she was dangling with one foot wedged tight.

"How in the world did you get in there?"

"I slipped off the gate," she wailed.

The stubble was left standing until spring, and after the furrows were upturned the soil collected moisture until the seeding time in the fall.

The chinking of Will's ax at the shrinking woodpile and the chant of his auctioneering awakened me. He felt the calm of the morning as he stepped over the high sill of the barn by four o'clock and hollered, "Whoa!" He had the hay and chopped wheat in the mangers for the draft horses by five o'clock. He "curried out" the salty smell of new sweat from their curved necks and trimmed their heavy fetlocks the night before, after they had rolled in the lot and blown the dust from their nostrils.

As soon as he had new bedding hay in the stalls, he came up the path, that connected the house and the barn, with Simon

6 Large horse-drawn combines, adapted to negotiating steep slops, replaced the headers and the stationary steam threshers operated by Jim Adams, Charlie Losey and Nordyke.

and Snip to the kitchen where the family lived, worked and played.

The yellow cat contentedly purred before the old black kitchen range, with a hearth of tin, a water tank to fill and a shelf above them all. It gave out heat that made the room warm and cozy. The feeble flames of the clean coal oil lamp on the table filled the room with a poor light. The delicious smell of fresh made applejack floated through the kitchen door.

"Hot cakes, eggs, bacon and coffee with last night's cream," I announced in a sleepy voice.

"Is there anything else you want for breakfast, Will?"

"You could give me some applejack," he said quickly.

After breakfast he harnessed each horse by slipping a padded collar over his head, buckling a set of hames with two brass knobs around the collar, pulling the pole strap between the front legs and snapping it under the belly, hooking the straps from the crupper into the tugs and attaching the britchen that went around the back legs to the tugs.

Holding the hinged bit against the horse's teeth, he slipped it into the horse's mouth, drew the bridle over the ears, threaded the throat latch, locked the lines into the bits, rolled them around the hame knobs and laced the spreaders that went from bit to bit to hold them all together.

Slack tugs slapped the sides of the heavy horses as they clopped across the shambling wooden bridge and pawed their way to the top of the mountain behind the house. His faith, like the mountain, pointed upward toward the realization of a dream that lightened his load and he looked unto the hills for his strength.

At the plow he clicked the butt chains—that always jingled —to the ends of the singletrees that were attached to the doubletrees, that hitched to the plow.

"Holding lines in your hands and being pulled by the team

as you walk through the soft loess is a feeling that goes too deep for human words," he remarked suddenly.

"What is it that you like so much about it?" Alec Teade tossed back.

Alec was burning off the heavy stubble.

"Each of these sixteen-hundred pound horses has his own traits. They tend to stand and feed together around the pasture hill. Jake, a dapple gray is high-lived, and always has his head up—he has an affinity for Dan, the bay Belgian, that is very steady. Bell and Blaze, the smaller bays with a small white star and a full blaze in the face, are fast trotters. Bonnie and Lady, the taller dark, brown-black mares with sleek coats, hesitate to give you enough room in the stall to harness them, and Maud and Queen are always ready to pull because Queen watches everything that I am doing. I like to hear their whinny of excitement. I like the way they work together as a team."

As soon as the heads had some kernels in them, there came the rustling, murmuring of wind swept fields of wheat.

The growing season from the last occurrence of a thirty-two degree freeze in the spring and the first such occurrence in the fall or from the middle of May to September twenty-third was at its height.

"I'll lay out the field and cut the hay today," said Will eagerly. "I'll be in early for dinner."

"What team are you going to use on the mower?" I asked elaborately.

"Buck and Pearl can pull the five-foot sickle mower," he said finally.

As the notched sickle slipped back and forth in the brass drill head, the golden grain fell in neat swathes inside the five-foot wire fence around the field and up the draws.

"Rake it up and dump it into windrows with the buckrake, Cleve," he said as Cleve Lowman rode into the field.

The buckrake had two high wheels with metal spokes and

oval tines set six inches apart that raised up when the hand lever was pushed forward.

"We will use pitchforks to shock the hay out of the windrows," Will commented. "Tomorrow you can pitch up and I will load the headerbox."

He drove the low side of the headerbox next to the shady end of the barn, wrapped the lines around the Jacob staff, set the wagon brake, pulled the fork down with the trip rope and set the fork into the load.

"Go ahead!" he called at last.

After hooking the cable into the singletree that was attached to the derrick cart and starting the horse to pulling up the load, the derrick driver cried, "Get up!" in response. The loaded fork tripped and slid along on the track in the top of the barn. Will hung onto the rope until it got to the part of the barn where he wanted to drop the hay and then he pulled the rope.

"Let her go," he chanted.

The horse always felt this loosing of the cable and started turning, so the alert driver caught the hook and unfastened it before the fork man started pulling back on the fork and tensing the cable. The horse circled to go back to the barn to rest until the next pull.

Thump! The right wheel of the cart veered out to the right and the cart fell to the ground. The stacker in the mow, who was pitching the hay to the sides of the barn, came out to see what the derrick driver wanted.

"If you can tell me how you did that, you can hook the cable to the singletree without the cart for the rest of the haying season!" he said, chuckling.

Two of the hayhands had taken the nut off the wheel at the noon hour.

As dusk was settling over the valley and a gentle breeze was whispering through the field of ripened grain, Will came over the brow of the hill with a load of hay. The wheels cramped, pitching the wagon down the hill. The hired man, who was riding on top of the load, went sprawling under the fence on his hands and knees. Will went out over the front of the box hanging onto the lines.

The team broke loose and raced down the circular road to the lower gate.

I scrambled through the walnut grove convulsing with fright, gripping my hand, contracting the muscles in my neck, grasping for breath, and uttering my feelings audibly. My strength was ebbing away.

The men, leaving the box, came down to get the horses. Thelma, Willma and Violet were crying.

"Well," he drawled, "We're free!"

His brusque words gave me confidence.

"I've always feared that point," I said stubbornly.

The children embraced their father. We came back to the house and he took the milk buckets to the barn.

"Nobody was hurt, Mother," he insisted in a thin voice as he poured the warm fresh milk into the bowl of the Blue Bell cream separator. Under the bowl were two spouts, one for cream and the other for milk. The children liked to watch the milk flow into the buckets and eat some of the foam that formed on top of the bucket. They could turn the handle after their father got it started. Usually their part was to take the disks out and put them on a wire that had a loop handle, wash all the parts and put it back together.

The cream flowed into a five-gallon cream can that we took to town every week to the Colfax Creamery. The creamery man took a sample with a small cup on a long metal handle, tested it for butter fat, and paid us accordingly. Cream sales decreased after 1940. Sales steadily dropped from 187,582 pounds of butterfat produced in 1940 to 117,138 pounds in 1959 in Whitman County.

We ate an early dinner. Then Will went to sleep in the big leather chair and Thelma on the big black leather tufted couch. The wooden stairway steps echoed back the sound of his tired feet as he carried her, crumpled comfortably against him, to her bed upstairs. Willma still slept in the downstairs trundle bed and Violet with me.

Soft winds were blowing, and the wheat was bursting forth, when we began getting things ready for the cookhouse that we took in the field with the stationary thresher.

"You can help me wash the blue and white granite dishes, Thelma," I said sternly.

"I'll dry them, Mother, and stack them on the worktable under the cupboard, so you can put them up," she said musingly.

I was rinsing the dishes on the stove with hot water from the tank. When we had finished, I said, "I'll wash the oilcloth on the tables and you can do the benches between the tables, that serve as seats over the bins where the dry food and cooking utensils are stored."

"We will fill all of the salt, pepper, sugar and syrup containers and you can put one on each table. The stainless steel flatwear goes into the drawers of the worktable."

"That's where I put them," was the reply.

The cookhouse had a door in each end, three tables along each side, an aisle down the middle and three-inch boards in the floor, imprinted with nails or spikes, on the men's shoes. Canvass flys on each side were held up by wooden props, and the windows were screened. A stove, a work table, a cupboard and a hot water tank were arranged in the front end. Four extended wheels were dropped in holes to keep the cookhouse from rolling. Steps that latched to the cookhouse, went up from either end.

Each field had "running water" from a tiled well, cased up and piped out to a big watering trough. The men dipped water from a barrel below the trough for washing their hands and face. Single towels were hung on the fence and washed every-day.

They had quaffed from the well's cool water before coming to the cookhouse. The water pail thumped against the jaws of the pump when they moved the handle up and down mak-ing a hollow squeaking sound. As the pressure built up, deep groans were followed by a trickle of water. Then suddenly a big flowing swoosh filled the bucket that hung over the knob on the spout of the pitcher pump. After the harvesters fin-ished eating, they stretched out on the immortal grass to rest before going back to the field.

The grasshoppers made a rasping sound while they jumped ahead of us as we went through the orchard in the early after-noon. We picked up the cherries that were half hidden in the uncut, unobstrusive grass.

"Someone likes crab apple jelly as well as we do," I ven-tured to say. "Look! They have stripped the tree."

"Oh, look Mother, the old woman's had a colt!" Willma shouted.

"It's Lady that has the colt," I laughed and she looked surprised.

Standing on a stepladder under the tree, I had my bucket about a third full when a big green and white snake swung around the branch and moved toward my bucket. The chil-dren, who had also crossed on the plank from the bank into the tree, had their aprons filled. We melted like shadows through the trees, grateful to get to the house with just enough cherries for our own use.

"Thump, thump," the excitement of harvest was here, when we could hear in the distance the whirring wheels of the Fairbanks Morse, a deisel oil engine Will used to drive the separator. The crew had gathered in their blue overalls with forks, canteens, tobacco and straw hats. They had hauled the separator and trap wagon to the field, dug in the cook-house and headerboxes, tapped the oil barrels, whistled at the horses and were cutting Mack's barley.

Will didn't come and didn't come! It was midnight so my brother Frank, who was visiting with me, went up to the setting to find him under the engine trying to replace a part he had removed to "oil up." Frank King liked nothing better than to take anything apart and put it back together again.

"I think it goes this way, Will!" he suggested.

It was breaking daylight before they got the engine running again, so they worked all day without sleep.

This engine had big heavy flywheels. The walls of the cylinders were very strong. It did not have spark plugs or a carburetor.

"What makes her go?" queried Frank.

"The air goes into the cylinders as the piston moves down," explained Will. "The piston moves up and squeezes the air into a small space. Compressing the air makes it very hot. Then a powerful pump squirts a little fuel oil into the cylinder. The air is so hot that the oil explodes and forces the piston down. The piston then moves up and forces out the waste gases that escape through the exhaust. The piston moves the connecting rod that turns the crankshaft which in turn revolves the flywheel."

After harvesting for thirty days, Will hitched Jute and Daisy, leaders, Bird and Beck, wheelers, and Ras and Jen, the swing team, to the wheat wagon and trailer to haul the wheat to Penawawa.

On a return trip Will wrapped his lines around the Jacob staff on the jockey box, and got down to give Aunt Mina Daniels a box of peaches from the Pierce orchards. After taking the box into the house, he was making change for Aunt Mina when the team started to run.

"They are running away," he said bitterly as he caught the

back of the wagon, threw the purse into the jockey box and let the money ricochet. Bracing his feet against the wagon bed, he whipped the team and made them run all the way up the canyon.

"Is someone sick at your house?" Aunt Anna Chamberlain called and asked. "I saw Will going up the road in a keen run."

"We are all fine, but I wonder what has happened!" I speculated.

Sweaty mules with loping ears sucked up a goodly store of water from the trough. Unsnapping the crupper, hames and hip straps, he hung the harness—which had recently been dipped in oil to keep it from cracking—over the pegs behind the mules. The excited mules dragged the halter chains across the mangers, thumped their big hooves on the hard ground and nibbled at the remaining wisps of hay. Flies buzzed through the doors, and the light from the late afternoon sun filtered through the cracks of the barn radiating across their dusty backs.

He came to the house grinning enormously, "They'll never run again! You can bet on that!" he said. Then he told us what had happened. The joy of common toil was in his heart though his arms ached from fighting the eight mules to keep them under control.

The last week in September, Art Stone started drilling the wheat—treated with blue vitral to kill the smut—into the ground. The drill box was divided and each section lifted up for filling.

"Shall I carry a half-sack on the drill for refilling as I'm going around the hill?" Art asked quickly.

"Just until I finish treating," Will confided.

From the pipes in the bottom of the drill box the wheat fell between two disks that furrowed the ground.

After dividing each sack of seed in half and dipping it into a vat of diluted blue vitral, Will set the treated wheat back on a platform to drain and dry. He then loaded it on a wagon and parceled it out in the field at intervals that were convenient for keeping the drill box filled.[7]

"The narrower the hitch the more power you have," I remarked to my husband, "Isn't that right?"

"That is the reason why I rigged the plow team out four and four, but eight abreast can pull the drill and harrow."

The wind yanked at my dress as I watched.

"I'll follow you with six sections of harrow, Art," he said. "The ground is pretty soft so I'll only set the levers in the third notch of the rachets of each section." The freshly harrowed ground felt cool beneath his feet. Into the draws deep dusty shadows were beginning to creep before the two men loosened the butt chains and started to the house with the teams.

"Don't you have a horse to ride?" asked Art.

"I'll ride Nedo tomorrow. He was lame today," he explained. "An Hungarian pheasant scooped its wings, rose from the stubble field, and sailed into the draw when I was riding out the pasture fence. Nedo jumped sideways and caught his foot in the wire."

Nedo was a tomato-red sorrel, saddle horse with a white streak in his mane and white feet. Will kept a low saddle of dark leather, that belonged to his father, on Nedo most of the time for doing anything he needed to do on the ranch. He loved to ride Nedo to the pasture to "bring up" the horses with Pinto our yellow-brown German shepherd, with a white ring around his neck. Pinto helped hunt coyotes, drive cattle,

---

7 Three thousand farms were in operation in Whitman County at this time. We had increased our farm to more than a thousand acres. This was still the average sized farm in 1959. Unit consolidation and mechanization has increased efficiency on these farms that are cash-grain operations, and some are non-resident operated.

"cut out" the horses and guard the house until he got very old. Then he would go behind the house and hide when Will called him to help with the stock.

In the stately old house standing among the sleeping hills beside the placid stream, I was holding the baby in the comfortable retreat of the old scarred chair with its rockers worn flat. The withering fields, where the crickets chanted their ode, had yielded fifty-five bushels of Elgin wheat per acre. The harvest had been gathered and stored by Hi Van Tine in the warehouse at Penawawa, and the fields that had been plowed under turned up a mellow sod.[8] The stream was brown with cattail sedge and milkweed seeds. The meadow, ablaze with goldenrod, harbored a pungent odor, and the willow leaves were dropping crisp and sear. The view of the distant hills was nourishment to an inner peace.

Will came to the door, and holding one arm outside said, "I ran my hand into the chop mill, Mother. Can you help me?" He brushed his thighs with his other mealy-white hand.

"I'll be with you in a minute," I told him.

"There's a lot of mice in those webby bins," he complained.

I laid the baby in the trundle bed, that had sliding sides. I fastened her in, tucked the covers under the mattress and told Thelma to watch her. Then, I hurried across the floor that was strewn with toys and met Will in the kitchen. His hand was bleeding, his face was white and he was in pain. His hand was torn down between the third and fourth fingers. I washed his hand, painted it with a disinfectant, and bound it with an unbleached muslin strip that drew tight.

I could hear the scrunch of the pebbles under Nedo's hooves long after he disappeared around the bend in the road where

---

8 This was the "intensive farming" period of agricultural development when fertilization and re-cropping increased the production on each piece of land. Yields varied from piece to piece and on different parts of each section.

the roots of the willow trees held the soil and helped to fill the floor of the valley.

In the yard the south wind strummed through the battered trees with their lattice work of boughs with buds unfolding themselves. The peonies hemmed in by the hedgerow of lilacs made it a lovely thing, surrounded by a white picket fence that was sagging here and there. The image that lingers deep within my mind of that crooked fence and the smell of the lilacs in the rain, will always be a part of the place.

The children—Thelma 10, Willma 6, Violet 4 and I— were perched on the steps of the front porch and Will was slouching in the circular-backed, willow rocker resting against its round low arms. We were looking to the north across the hills new-greening.

Willma was handing me buttons from the old button box and I was sewing them on Violet's apron. The old button box was a link with the past. In it were buttons worn by my mother, sisters and grandmother.

"I bought two American Saddlers," he said, when I was at the Lewiston sale last week.

"What are their names?" I asked.

"Ruby and Flicker!" he said, "Chestnut sorrels, with light tails."

"I would like to join the Saddle Club."

"We'll do that and then you can ride Flicker in the Whitman County Parade next fall. I'll ride Ruby."

By fair time he had them gentled and had new saddles for both of them. Will had tooled breast straps and side straps to the stirrups. His bridle was tooled to match the breast strap, but his tapaders were a different design and he had a striped saddle blanket.

I had a complete matching set of leathers, with a martingale for a breast strap.

We wore black riding pants and black boots. My jacket

was white-fringed leather, his was white leather trimmed with silver buttons, laced on with tongs of leather. We both wore wide brimmed hats, gauntlet gloves and riding whips.

"Flicker is getting excited," I said. "She wants to throw her head."

"Rein her up and stay right beside me," he cautioned.

The excitement of the crowd caused the horses to whinny, sneeze, prance, swing and sway as we passed the grandstand and crossed the field.

After taking Ruby and Flicker home in the trailer, we went back to get Azalia. We had reached the bottom of the Wilcox hill, when we could hear the pounding of her back feet on the bottom of the trailer.

We stopped and Will went around to see what she was doing. She was reared up over the top of the car ready to come down through, stomping the floor with her hind feet. When she saw us get out of the car, she leaped into the road and landed on her side. He caught her by the halter and we managed to get her back into the trailer.

"Quiet now, girl! Easy, girl, easy!" he said stroking her lathered neck.

By driving very slowly we got her to the ranch gate and turned her into the meadow where the long legged killdeers were making mud-tracks among the clumps of blue flags. The tantalizing aroma of the yellow-centered dog fennel mingled with the warm smell of the freshly trodden green grass blades that were pushing up through the sod. The gentle breeze was wafting the fragrant scent of blue violets to our nostrils as we walked to the house along the winding brown trails where the land could kiss our feet.

"I'm going to break out the pasture hills below," he said.

"They should yield very high," I commented. "They have never been planted."

The next morning I called to Will, "Come here and see

Azalia! She is standing on the outside of the fence! How did she get out?"

We had finished our breakfast so we hurried out to see what had happened.

When we got to the gate he said, "She has been in the fence." Her foot was bleeding, but she could walk on it.

"Bring me some of the salve from Dr. Cummings, while I snub her up," he suggested.

Her leg was healing so there were not going to be any scars left. We had given her a treatment and Will had gone up on the hill to help Tom Brannon pull the stubble out of the plow. After Tom went on around the hill, Will rode back to the house and tied Prince in the south side of the barn.

As we were walking across the lawn toward the house, I said, "I'll go in and fix the lunch." I went around the house pushing off the touch of Zeke's delighted tongue. Zeke was an Australian shepherd, a sheep dog, with a glass eye that we got from Uncle Ira when he lived at John Major's.

"Come quick," I called. "The barn is afire."

The hot fast-burning fire spread so quickly through the barn that he couldn't get Prince out.

"It's gone mother," he flashed. "Call the Wilcox fire department, maybe we can save the rest of the buildings." And we did, but we lost eighteen tons of fine new hay, three saddles and harness for twenty-two head of horses.

With it went the memories of our best-loved friends—such as Leroy, a singlefooter, that we used to drive to the buggy. As long as you held the reins tight he would run harder all the time until you loosened them. One Sunday I drove him to the Grange Hall and tied him up. When we went out to get into the buggy, he started around the Grange Hall and around and around he went with Mr. Reidenauer pulling back on the reins. Myrtle, Thelma and I jumped in over the back seat when he came around the last time and after we loosened his reins he walked all the way home.

The last time that Will ran him down on the track at the old Fairgrounds at Colfax he hitched him to a cart. His hobbles broke in front of the grandstand and he lost his race. The whips used on the other horses seemed to make him nervous.

Smoky, purchased from Harvey Freeman, was a trick horse that would stand on the training posts with one foot on each one and open all the gates he came to. He was a smoky-gray with a white star on his face. He always wanted to be where Dad was. He would try to come in the shop when Dad was working there.

Chapter VI

ALONG THE SUSQUEHANNA RIVER

"I would like to go back and walk in on Hank!" Will mused.

"We could go on the train?" I questioned.

"We might go after the first of May," he decided.

"Let's do it; I'll call and find out about fares."

When we got to Washington, D. C., Henry was working in the yard.

"Would you have a room to rent?" Will asked him.

"No," Henry answered, "we haven't any rooms here."

"Well, would you have a room for a brother?"

Tears started in Will's eyes and then Henry realized that he was his brother.

We went into the house and Marian came to meet us.

"Here are Will and Olive," Henry told her.

Doris came home from the Gas Company office.

"Aunt Olive and Uncle Will! When did you get here?"

"We came on the 11:00 o'clock," I said.

Will and Henry visited about their family that lived in Dushore, Pennsylvania, where they were born and lived until 1883 when they came by train to Washington.

"Do you know when Grandfather Philip Hugh Miller came to America?" Will interrogated.

"I have a record of his arrival on the *Thomas and William* ship at New York on June 20, 1837 from Belfast, Roll 34, List 502. His name appears on the passenger list as Hugh Miller, age 25," related Henry. "Would you like to see it?"

119

"I surely would!" Will assured him.

"This is his diary telling about the trip," said Henry as he handed it to Will to read.

———

"On this crisp dawn, a fresh breeze was blowing. The hills moved away with majesty, and the towering clouds twisted with violence. The river slashed through the meadows that were flooding with the light of day. The boat slithered from the west end of the dock that arched out from the trees to the water's edge. The boat, the *Thomas and William,* plied its stolid way past the lights that pricked out from the unexpectedly steep-roofed houses along the shore.

"The ever retreating horizon was visible for many miles as the boat navigated the waters of the crooked variable river.

" 'Do you like to see the breakers rolling in from the sea?' I asked.

" 'They tune out the rustling of the wind in the trees along the banks,' answered Patrick McNalley.

" 'Look over there where they overflow the land and frost it with foam.' I taunted.

"As the ship made a steady northing, the cry of the sea birds sounded near. Beyond the new horizon lay the land in which my ancestors built their new homes.

"The towering sails, white above the sea glare, moved past the Emerald Isle.

" 'There is something about the ocean and how the ships leave the Irish shore that intrigues me,' I pondered.

"As the emigrant ship nosed in to tie up at New York, the breeze carried a deep woodsy smell that came from beyond the blue haze where the trees made a line against the sky.

" 'Our food basket is getting low,' ventured Patrick.

" 'We have been drinking this slimy water for more than four weeks now,' I bantered. 'It tasted good the first week out.' "

"None of his family came with him?" Will asked.

"He came from Ireland with Irish friends!" Henry assured him. "Some Miller families came to Berks County in Pennsylvania in 1720 and migrated up the Susquehanna River the same as the Weavers, Hunsingers and Thrashers. He came to Sullivan County to join them, met Grandmother and built his home there." Henry explained.

Will continued reading the diary.

"On the inland farm to the north later owned by Anthony Middendorf, I homed up. This farm had been established by attacking this great hardwood forest of oak, ash, beech, hickory, walnut and cedar trees along the Susquehanna River with ax and saw, hacking out the material for the log cabin of rude, honest structure. It offered food, shelter, and warmth of a glowing fire.

"I helped to spread the well cultivated clearing further and further over the rolling hills.

" 'We will cut fence posts and rails from the cedar trees and enclose the land and cattle,' explained the nester.

"I tended the great log barn that kept the cattle warm in winter. I also cut and carried fireplace wood to the two-story stone house that had been built for the family, and the original log cabin where I bunked.[9]

---

9 William Penn visited the Rhineland in 1671. Stimulated by Penn and his agents, the Swiss and German people began to form companies and to acquire the necessary gear for the long and dangerous journey. They sailed down the Rhine to Rotterdam and thence to England, where they finally boarded what might be called the Pennsylvania German *Mayflower,* with their Bibles in their hands and their hearts filled with prayer. Francis Daniel Pastorious led this little party to Penn's City, "The City of Brotherly Love." There they founded Germantown, a suburb of Philadelphia which still has an individuality.

"The kitchen in the main house, where we ate our meals, had a wooden box to hold salt, hung by the fireplace. It was carved and decorated with a heart and tulips. Iron cooking pots hung on cranes over the fire, and long forks and utensils projected from the carved beam which made the shelf over the ten foot fireplace.

"The onion shoots that sprouted out of an old yellow and green vase that swung on chains from the ceiling were clipped for a taste of greens during the winter. A bank of dark brown earthenware stood on the window sill nearest the door. The children did not often get coins and when the bank was filled it was broken to free its contents. On the low shelves beneath the windows were numerous ceramic toys, water-whistles, miniature animals, a cock and hen, wind instruments, and doll dishes. Pierced ceramic plates lined the plate rail at the far end of the room.

"When the door of the pie cupboard stood open the air was filled with special flavor. As many as fifty pies were baked outdoors in an oven similar to the one used along the Rhine. They were baked in a flat earthenware dish that had a notched edge and curved rim.

" 'Mrs. John Hartzig is the hostess for a flax spinning party Friday evening, Philip,' said Mrs. Thrasher. 'Would you like to go over for the dancing in the evening and take some of the girls home with their spinning wheels?'

" 'Could I take the team we have been using to haul the clay up from the meadow to the mill?' I asked.

" 'There is enough clay to keep the mill running for at least

---

They were devout, honest, simple folk prepared for hardship and used to work. They wanted to build permanent homes. They bought good land and everyone worked, for the land and the land alone must support them. The earth repaid them. Nothing was too much trouble, no day too long. Ref.: *Folk Art of Rural Pennsylvania* by Frances Lichten, p. 6.

two days before we will need to use the horses again,' explained Mrs. Thrasher.

"The mill ground the clay for the making of pottery. It had a group of knives set in an upright post that revolved in a stationary tub, operated by a long sweep to which a horse was attached. The clay was sprinkled with water, and the horse started around. I kept the horse in motion and stopped when the clay was finely ground.

"After the clay was moulded into one-hundred pound blocks, I helped to haul and store it away from the danger of freezing in a cellar behind the workshop.

"I gathered dust from the road with a wheelbarrow, put it through a fine sieve and poured it into a pot. The pots were stored for the dusting of the work bench when the clay was molded into plates.

"After a long week, the night of the party arrived.

"Mrs. Hartzig introduced me to her granddaughter, Salina. We danced together most of the evening.

" 'May I take you home, Miss Hartzig!' I asked when the dancing was nearly over.

" 'You certainly may,' said Salina blushingly.

"A swift glance from her steel blue eye was alive with emotion. My dream of Salina was strong and growing stronger as we rode through the glen. I would win my dream, and it was a wonderful feeling. At last I had a chance to tell her of my love. Into the beautifully patterned fabric of our family life, we began to weave the single threads. The fabric was fine.

"In her mind's eye, she saw every bed covered with colorful spreads, either of her own weaving or a pattern of her own choice when she informed her parents of her forthcoming marriage. Some blue and white coverlets with a flax warp, and wool, dyed a strong blue with the precious indigo, used as the woof, were woven by her family in the home, but they were only of geometrical patterns. She also got to choose a pattern from the sample book of the professional weaver who traveled over the rough roads to each household. The background of her design was alternated stripes with the pattern done in brilliant yarns of every hue.

" 'The homespun linen in your dower chest will make nice *toell pjrely,*' said Catharine Hartzig.

" 'Cross-stitch with red cotton thread would make it easy to count the threads between stitches.'

" 'I would like to embroider Barbi's pattern of the two ladies in wide hoopskirts and the flowers,' Salina said. 'Then I will sign my name and put on the date.'

"Salina Hartzig's family were descendants from the early settlers, arriving from Berne, Switzerland—that country of butter and woodcarvers, who thought that 'printed butter' brought better prices. Their daughter must be skilled in the care of milk and its transformation into butter, so they presented her with several beautifully carved butter molds.

"A blessing was carved for the lintel of our house which was built characteristically into a hillside with the lower portion used as the spring house. The stones were set in random size and held together by lime mortar burned from the limestone rocks by placing them in a big kiln.

"The chimneys were built toward the end of the shingled roof to accommodate fireplaces. The 'watertable,' a narrow slanting shingled roof, a feature of the palatinate house that carried all the way around the house over the first story windows was reduced to a heavy type of cornice. The small window just under the roof gave light to a bedroom in the loft. We hung blinds instead of wooden shutters to close over the French windows at night. The shingles were nailed on the roof when the points of the moon were down.

"Grass, which had ascended the eminences and softened their contours, tempered the climate along the banks of the Susquehanna River in Pennsylvania. Cattle that grazed on the upland came to kneel and drink from the river's slushy banks. From the low-growing trees that flanked the river, birds swung out and swooped across the landscape to break the spell of the countryside. Fleecy white clouds often deleted the blue from the sky. Gentle breezes wafted the cool damp river smells and the pungency of the weeds along the road through the open windows of our stone house in Cherry Township, Sullivan County, Pennsylvania."

"Was Father, Augustus Miller, born there?" Will asked.

"Ann, Louisa, Augustus, Henry, Louis, Naomi, Julietta, Guilford and Albert were born there," confirmed Henry.

"Is this house still standing?" Will questioned.

"The cellar is still being used for the lagering of beer," said Henry. "He tells a little further on how he made his beer."

"When I went on the rich land that had lain under the thickest forest, I intended to stay there. I had waited a long time to plan for myself a permanent home. Like the dwellings of the Rhineland, the stone farmhouse added a note of solidity to the angled patterns of farms.

"Work was good and waste was sinful.

"On the gently rounded, cultivated hills of many sizes, I planted barley, a cereal that can be fermented and flavored with hops to make beer. I built a cellar of stone for the cooling and 'lagering' of beer. The water from the springhouse I treated to eliminate mineral salts. The barley was roasted and mashed. The cone of the female hop, which we picked free of leaves and stem, and dried, was added for flavor and to prevent bacterial action. Then we added yeast to cause the sugars to become alcohol. The beer settled to the bottom. It was heated to thirty-seven degrees for fermentation.

"When the children were getting big enough to help, I sowed three acres thickly with flax seed in late April. It grew to three feet and had a mass of lovely blue blossoms in June. The blossoms turned into seeds, the seeds ripened, and the stalks became woody and hollow. We harvested it in July, by pulling the plants up by the roots, piling them into small bundles and tying them with straw. The bundles were laid on the floor of the 'bank barn,' which had stone ends and was built into a south-facing bank.[10] The foundation floor of this barn was warm for the stock and the wagonload of flax bundles could be driven in on the loft floor above. Corn shocks were stacked against the exposed parts of the foundation.

" 'Weight the roots on the threshing floor with a plank and beat the seed heads before you spread the stalks out in the meadow, Augustus,' I told my son. 'Henry will help you.'

"After the 'boon' or outside covering of the stalks had rotted in the meadow we brought them to the 'flax-break.' Salina, Ann and Louisa heated the bundles over a grate set over a slow burning fire before we put them on the 'flax-break.' In autumn, the sound of our 'flax-break' and smoke from the fires drifted across the valley.

"The third time we bundled the flax we carried it to a shed where the younger children, Louisa and Naomi, helped to take out the last seeds and fragments of 'boon' with a 'swingle,' a sharpened wooden knife with rounded edges.

"Salina, Ann, Louisa, Naomi and Julietta drew the flax through the 'hatchel,' or graduated iron combs which took out the 'tow' or snarls. The snarls were saved for rough weaving. From the 'hatchel' we twisted the smooth, blond and shining strands into neat spiral hanks. These were tied and hung from

---

10 A traveling artist drew barn symbols or hex signs on the loft of the barn with a huge wooden compass and painted them. The hex signs were supposed to protect the barn from lightning and the livestock from harm resulting from the machinations of witches.

the attic rafters and we all worked from Halloween to Christman to spin the twists into thread.

" 'Linsey-woolsey,' made of flax and wool, after dyeing was pressed for the making of petticoats, as well as rough work clothes."

"Father's brother, Henry Miller, went into the Palouse country in Washington first?" ventured Will, when he had finished reading the diary of Great Grandfather Philip Hugh Miller, who died in Dushore, Pennsylvania on July 4, 1871, and was buried beside the Thrasher church in the Old Zion Lutheran Cemetery before his family went West.

"That great expanse of grassland, the river that drained most of it, and the Indians that lived there had been named 'Pelouse,' by the French fur traders," related Hank.

"This letter written to his mother is dated 1875," said Hank as he handed it to Will.

"Where the Little Penawawa Creek 'breaks out' along the long scraggly slopes that widen toward their source and stretch into the blue haze, I, Henry Miller, in 1874, built a board and batten house, made of wide boards with their joinings covered with a narrow one, eight pane windows, narrow-cased doors, and a center chimney.

"The bolting, bumping, and thumping ride of the Conestoga wagon, stagecoach, and saddled cayuse brought me to Colfax in Whitman County in the State of Washington from Pennsylvania.[11]

---

11 The best of these wagons were made in the Conestoga Valley in Lancaster County, Pennsylvania, and used by the farmers to make trips to Philadelphia to barter for their salable goods, butter and flour. They were used also for carrying freight and passengers across the country before the railroads were built. Flax, produced on the farms, underwent a complete transformation into a fabric for a "Wagon Cloth" that was stretched and fastened over the circular framework above the blue and

"The Conestoga wagon that I started west in was really an inn, stocked with beds and food supplies, flour, flax and canteens. It had a sway in the middle so the supplies would slide toward the center of the wagon where the hard trail became rough. Milk in the canteens turned to butter by night due to the vibration of the wagon wheels over the rocks and ruts on the trail. When one trail became too rough the driver turned out and made a new road.

"The pony express, carrying mail—and accompanied by Felix Warren, a veteran of the western trails—brought me from Walla Walla to Colfax, and continued on to Lewiston, Idaho, and up the Clearwater River to Grangeville, Idaho.[12]

"I applied for possession of my land to the United States Patent Office, January 16, 1884, Homestead Certificate No. 531, Application 99 in the United States of America, Pursuant to the Act of Congress approved May 20, 1862.

"To secure Homesteads to actual settlers on the Public Domain, and the acts supplemental there-to the Claim of Henry L. Miller has been established and duly consummated in conformity to Law for the West Half of the South West Quarter, the North East Quarter of the South East Quarter of Section Twenty-two in Township fifteen, North Range forty-two East of Willamette Meridan in Washington Territory containing one hundred and sixty acres of mineral rights.

---

vermillion wagon beds. Lids fastened on by wrought iron hinges and hasps, made by the local smiths, strengthened the tool boxes and ornamented them.

12 The Warrens had lived at Walla Walla since 1865. Felix Warren's stagecoaches increased until they covered an area of five hundred miles, employing two hundred horses, and a large force of drivers. Sol Warren, his brother, married my sister, Julietta Miller. Mary Warren married Henry Hart Spaulding of Almota, whose father, Henry Harmon Spaulding, directed the people in the ways of peace and Christianity. Henry Harmon Spaulding was buried in the shifting sands of the Snake River with not even a wooden slab to mark his grave, which cannot even now be definitely located.

"In testimony whereof, Chester A. Arthur, President of the United States of America have caused these letters to be made patent, and the seal of the General Land Office to be hereunto affixed.

"I received title to my home and my land in 1884 after which time I sold it to my brother, Augustus Miller, for $1200.

"When Augustus Miller built his house across the hill, my house became the first Miller school."[13]

"Uncle Henry Miller died the year after Dad bought the place?" questioned Will.

"Yes, and Grandmother Salina Hartzig Miller and Uncle Guilford homesteaded the lower meadow and lived there,"

---

13   Maida Templeton Harrison cherishes the memory of her school days here with Faye Templeton, Ivy Hanna, Ortis Johnson, Ralph Johnson, John Miller, Will Miller, Ellery Miller and Joe Adams.

Leonard Abrams was the first teacher that I had in the Miller school, and the term was one month. Cora Adams was the second teacher we had and she later taught in the Willow Creek and Hickman schools. Lester Still, Anna Stinson, Miss Nalder—sister of Frank Nalder of Pullman, who was born in Australia and partly raised there—and Miss Ida Gustafson taught in our school. Ida boarded with the Gus Miller family.

The desks were double and homemade. I had to sit in the back so I could get my knees under the double desks. The seats raised up and you had to get in and sit down and then push the seat down. The desks were slanted with a shelf underneath to hold the books. We had a reader, arithmetic, geography, history, physiology and Penmanship Copy book. We had penmanship for five minutes every afternoon. In art class we transferred and colored pictures. We decorated the walls with the transfer pictures to get ready for our first Christmas tree. The Schlotthauer children came after sundown and snitched some of them. The old pot-bellied stove stood in the middle of the floor. We all stood around it with our coats on until, as sometimes happened, someone put a rubber on it and we all moved away. We filled the stove with coal and stirred it to keep it from blowing up. We had a good time and we didn't think anything about it. Our parents didn't mind as long as we got to school.

The name of the school was changed when it was moved to the property of Mrs. Anna Templeton, my mother. Laura Greer and Georgia Saxon were our teachers for several years. Will Miller finished under John W. Duff and I completed the eighth grade under Mrs. Bill Brown.

replied Henry. "They grew some of the first wheat in Whitman County, and hauled it to the warehouse at Penawawa."

"I remember how they planted it in the spring," said Will. "Don't you recall how they talked about how much better crop they had when they planted Turkey Red?"

"We were sewing Pacific Bluesteam when I started studying at the Washington State College Experiment Station at Pullman, Washington with Dr. Spillman."

"How did you happen to come to Washington, D. C.?" asked Will.

"I had studied seven years with him at the experimental station when he asked me to accompany him to Washington, D. C. and work with him here," explained Hank.

"I will take you over to the Agricultural Department and show you where I worked with Dr. Spillman for over forty years," offered Henry.

Henry took Will and I to the building to see the offices and the museum where Lindbergh's plane is displayed. Henry, Jr. and Isabelle drove us to Maryland through the hills where we saw tobacco farms, and passed the Government Experiment Station, where they were raising hogs. Doris and Kal visited the home of George Washington at Mount Vernon and Washington's Monument with us.

When we came home to Colfax, the wheat—Federation, king of all the grasses—had stooled on the slopes of our Palouse hills. The native grasses, grazed off by the cattle in the late fall, had blanketed the meadow and the hill behind the house. Festering weeds along the edge of the Penawawa Creek had delayed the loess suspended in the current and heaped it in swales of bubbly, muddy slime. The fields were awash with the run off from melting snow.

We continued in farming until Mr. Miller's death April 30, 1958.

I own the Will Miller farm, and operate it by hiring Dave

Baldwin to do the custom farming. The Ellery Miller Farm is owned and operated by Pauline Miller, her son Marshall Miller and other heirs. The John Miller Farm is owned and operated by Dr. James Miller. Each farm has for many years used the varieties of wheat developed at the Washington State University including the latest, "Nu Gaines," which is believed to be a little more rust resistant, have a little better milling quality and have a high yield about the same as the regular Gaines.

Acreage limitations by the Federal Wheat Acreage Allotment Program, initiated in 1954, to 350,000 acres in the county are being compensated for by the use of fertilizers and the high yielding "Nu Gaines." (Floyd Hopkins, manager of the McGregor Co., fertilizes our crop land in September.)

Ninety-one percent of the acreage fertilized in Whitman County was in wheat and barley in 1965. Thirty-one million bushels of wheat were produced in Whitman County in 1967, the largest single wheat producing county in the United States.

Landowners are farming additional land for cash which is known as custom farming. In 1967, 24,400,000 bushels of cereal grains were transported from Whitman County by the Union Pacific, the Great Northern, the Northern Pacific and the Spokane, Portland and Seattle railways; by truck over a fine network of county, state and two U. S. Highways 195, and 295 respectively; and via the Snake and Columbia River System to Seattle, Tacoma, Spokane, Portland and markets to the East, as well as to some coastal and foreign markets.

Average annual tonnage to be carried on the lower Snake River after completion of the four dams, constructed to deepen the river for slack-water navigation, is estimated in excess of four million shipping tons. Ice Harbor was dedicated May 9, 1962 by Lyndon Johnson, speaker. The John Day Dam was dedicated September 7, 1968, with Hubert Humphrey as speaker. Slack-water navigation will be possible from the

Pacific Ocean for 470 miles up the Columbia and Snake Rivers to Lewiston-Clarkston after the completion of Lower Monumental, Little Goose and Lower Granite.

Barges will be used because they are more economical, can carry a large load, require smaller crews and are loaded and unloaded more easily. However, to distant points such as Hong Kong, Toyko and the Phillipines, they cannot compete with the ocean-going grain ships. They will be less costly to Alaska and California.

A special floating terminal vessel in the Portland area, which would move in between a grain-filled river barge and an ocean-going ship, would be less costly than the regular unloading at a grain elevator and later discharging to a ship. Designing of portable shoreline truck unloading facilities, floating storage barges capable of loading river barges and other mobile river-going devices is underway.

Maida Harrison called this afternoon and brought clippings from her scrapbook telling about the steamboats that ran on the Snake River when we were little girls playing in our Grandmother Mary Fincher's yard at Penawawa.

Do you remember the day when we were swinging high enough so that we could see up the river and your swing caught on mine and tore my knee cap? We burst into the house and you fell and hit your doll's head against the big stove!

Grandma was bandaging my knee and you said, "Put a mustard plaster on my doll's head and it will be all right."

"I think I have a new head for your doll," grandmother said consolingly as she helped you pick up the pieces.

"Who was the man who took the first steamboat up the river, Grandmother?" I asked.

"Come children, we will sit in the big rockers and I will tell you the story of the river boats.

"Captain E. W. Baughman, the first man to navigate a steamboat up the Snake River—none of which is more dangerous—stood erect at his wheel. He could only tell by the looks of the water where the channel was the deepest. Daylight flooded the canyon on October 24, 1858, as the *Colonel Wright* slithered up through the very deep and narrow channel and lined over the rapids.

"A long cable, securely fastened above the rapids, with a large barrel on its end to carry it downstream was in readiness when the *Colonel Wright* came to the lower end of the rapids. The barrel was lifted to the prow and the cable placed upon the steamboat.

"The capstan then was put in motion, and the boat wound its way up the cable. When the top of the rapids was reached, the cable, with the barrel on the end, was thrown overboard, and the force of the current carried it downstream to be picked up on another trip.

"The *Colonel Wright,* built at the mouth of the Deschutes River, docked in April, 1859, at the Lewiston settlement, proving that the Snake River was navigable. The steamer made three trips a week and hauled freight for eighty dollars a ton.

"Going downstream, Captain Baughman reversed his motor and started the wheels going backwards. This threw a large volume of water under the boat and helped to carry it over the swift, shallow, Steptoe, O'dell, Pine Tree and Little Goose Rapids."

"How many boats went up the river?" we asked.

"Soon steamboats, owned by the Oregon Steam Navigation Company, held a monopoly on the river traffic with one boat going up the river and one down everyday. Twelve hundred dollars a month was paid 'by the dispensers' for the privilege of catering to the thirst of the traveling public who were mostly miners headed for the gold fields discovered in 1860, in the mountains east of Lewiston."

"What else did they have on the boats?"

"The sixteen steamers, called 'the wheat fleet,' carried

wheat, fruit and wool produced in Asotin, Garfield and Whitman Counties down the river which was dredged after 1880."

"Who were the captains on the other boats? Did they get very much money for taking the boats up the river?" Maida asked moving her rocker closer to Grandmother.

"The first captains employed by the company, that carried gold on the return trip down the river, received five hundred dollars a month in salary. Some of them were Captain Baughman and his sons, Captain John Stump, Captain Arthur Riggs, Captain W. P. Gray, Captain Works, Captain John E. Akins and Captain John E. Aims.

"The purser of the *Tenino,* second boat on the river turned in one thousand to four thousand dollars each trip. Captain John Stump took the first boat over the Celilo Falls, the *Okanogan,* which ran on the upper river until 1866. Captain W. H. Gray built the *Casadilla,* a sternwheeler of small power, in 1862, and operated the boat on the Clearwater to Lapwai, to Asotin, and later from Wallula to Priest Rapids. Captain Gray also built a passenger boat, *Nez Perce Chief,* in 1863. Her gold dust on October 29, 1863 was valued at three hundred and eighty-two thousand dollars. In 1865 Captain Thomas Stump attempted to take her to the upper Snake River. She was eight days going a distance of one hundred miles. He took the boat the furthest upstream and in 1870 went over the Tumwater Falls and the Cascades.

"The *Spray,* a small steamer built at the mouth of the Deschutes River, paid for herself three times during the first five months on the river.

"The *Yakima* or the *Owhee,* built in 1864 for the Oregon Steam Navigation Company, was a champion on the upper river. It was a handsome craft with twenty-five staterooms, sumptuously furnished, and a freight capacity of two hundred tons. The *Yakima* made a record run of forty-one hours and thirty-five minutes from Celilo to Lewiston.

"The *Almota,* built in 1876 at Celilo shipyards for the Lewiston run, carried a boatload of soldiers from Celilo to Lewiston in 1877 to reinforce General Howard's troops during the war with Chief Joseph. The one trip paid for the cost of building the boat.

"The *Annie Faxon,* launched in 1877, with Captain E. E. Baughman in command ran from Celilo to Lewiston until the completion of the railroad to Riparia in 1881. In 1887 the *Annie Faxon* was rebuilt for the Riparia-Lewiston run, and was in regular service until August 14, 1893, when she exploded her boiler, killing eight people. Among the survivors were Harry Baughman, Roger Morrisey, Captain J. E. Akins and Sage Akins of Lewiston.

"The *Spokane,* a light draft boat built in thirty-two days and six hours, in 1877, became a gunboat for General Howard to prevent the hostile Bannock Indians from crossing the Columbia River. It was outfitted with sacks of wool stood on end around the pilot house. Small apertures permitted Captain Stump to see to navigate. Prevented from crossing the Columbia, the Indians went back to the Grand Ronde. The *Spokane* was loaded with soldiers and piloted to the mouth of the Grande Ronde where the soldiers arrived in time to prevent a massacre. In 1882, the *Spokane* carried stone from Granite Point for a railroad bridge at Ainsworth.

"*John Gates, Harvest Queen, D. S. Baker,* 1878-79 were used during high water, until the railroad to Riparia was completed in 1881. The *John Gates* was condemned in 1890. Boat service from Celilo to Riparia was discontinued and the *Harvest Queen* was taken over the Cascades to Portland, Oregon.

"The *Lewiston,* constructed in 1894, in part from the cabin of the *John Gates,* was taken as far as Kamiah on a reconnoiter trip by Captain E. W. Baughman in May of 1896. While the trip was a success it was never repeated.

Frequently trips to Orfino were made. (The *Lewiston* was used on the upper Snake River until 1922 when it was destroyed by fire along with the *Spokane* when they were tied up at the Lewiston docks. These were the only two boats on the river, so the *H. M. Teal* from Portland was brought up for use until a new boat could be built.)

"The *New Lewiston,* the last boat in service for the O. W. R. & Co. was launched at Portland, on December 1st. It was 100 feet long, had a thirty-six-foot long beam and a sixteen-foot draught. The boilers developed three-hundred tons. She had a water filtering plant, electric lights, and compressed air steering gear. The latter device provided entertainment for the crew at night when the boat was tied up. It hauled grain across the Snake River above Asotin."

We spent many enjoyable hours with Grandmother. We always stayed as long as our mothers would let us, but this was the only time she told us about the boats.

"This article tells about the boats that were built later," Maida commented. "Would you like to read it?"

"I'll read it aloud," I suggested.

"The *Imnaha* built in 1903 at Lewiston for the mining interests at the mouth of the Imnaha River, successfully navigated the fifty-three miles for about a year carrying passengers, machinery and supplies. On her last trip while lining over Mountain Sheep Rapids, the cable became fowled in her wheel and she drifted back over the rapids striking the shore. Her crew got off but she was a total loss.

"The *Mountain Gem* replaced the *Imnaha* and was withdrawn from the upper Snake to handle wheat shipments at Asotin to Lewiston. The *Mountain Gem* made the first trip through the state portage road at Celilo in 1905, operated from Celilo to Pasco, in 1906, and then was placed under J. E. Akins, command for freight service from Lewiston to Riparia until June, 1907. Then the boat was sold to Seattle interests and was used in the Kennewick, White Bluff, and Hanford areas for several years.

"The *Inland Empire* and *Twin Cities* were built by the Open River Association in 1908, and they ran from Celilo to Lewiston, making connection with the *H. M. Teal* on the lower river run."

"Mother took me to Lewiston on the boat and when we started home the whistle sounded so loud that we all ran to the rail to watch the ship leave the shore," Maida recalled.

Chapter VII

BEYOND THE HORIZON

We were enjoying a Sunday drive through the Palouse farming country when we were surprised by a sudden change in the terrain. The highway curved left over the edge of the Snake River Gorge where the sundrenched, brown palisades extend in undulations back from the river above Almota. We had left the rich grain hills that rolled away to the far horizon and were negotiating the Almota grade that went around the hills like an Indian trail of steep descent with a town at its end.

We drove down into Almota to see the Jack Millers who lived in the old Spaulding Hotel. They invited us in to see what they called their "big house."

"Where are they going to put the Lower Granite Dam across the river?" I asked in a noncommittal voice.

"It will begin on the south shore and go toward the north, the powerhouse followed by the spillway, navigation lock and north abutment is different from the other three dams," Jack grinned as he explained. "It will be 3½ miles upstream from Almota."

"How high is it going to be?" I interrogated.

"The standardized dimensions of the downstream navigation locks will be carried through at Lower Granite with the height of the gate dependent upon its normal pool level of 738 feet," he clarified.

"How will it effect fishing upstream?"

"There will be one fish ladder with a slope ratio of 1 to

10 that will allow two-way passage for anadromous fish," he assured me.

"What about the power output?"

"The powerhouse design of the Lower Granite will take advantage of the late improvements in generator design. It will allow for greater individual generator kilowatt output than specified at Little Goose, Lower Monumental and Ice Harbor." He elucidated further.

"Levee work necessary on both shores of the Clearwater, at Lewiston, Idaho and between Lewiston and Clarkston in order to tame the mighty Snake River was started during the summer of 1965.

"Above Almota the entire course of the river will be switched. The Snake River will go along the south bank of the island while the north channel is enlarged to hold the entire river flow, and after the cofferdams are built, the river will go on the other side of the island. Behind the coffer-dams will be a waterfree space where the actual concrete will be poured. Two diversion dikes and the island will leave the Whitman County side free of water. Pumps will pump out seepage. Six and one half million yards of dirt excavated from the north side will be deposited so as to build an air-field and some of it will be stored on the island for work on the cofferdam. Between the two cofferdams will be a 1700 foot wall of steel that is 45 feet high. It will be made of 32 cells of connected interlocking piling, pounded to bedrock in a circle around the pattern and then filled with gravel inside. It will also be packed with bags of cement along the channel side to form a solid barrier against the water. Each sheet of piling is 50 feet long, 14 inches wide; and the diam-eter of each cell is 51 feet."

"How did they get the machinery in?" I persisted.

"Rumbling wheels and chugging engines brought in two scrapers with a capacity of 38 cubic yards of earth each, four

25-yard scrapers, five bulldozers and one Cat-16 on the Camas Prairie Railroad."

"Will the Camas Prairie Railroad be replaced from Riparia to Lewiston?" I asked anxiously.

"Yes, the railroad will be re-located as near as possible to its present location along the Snake River and the Columbia at government expense, which is less than the cost of buying out the trackage in order to abandon service. The railroad will continue to be competitive to the shipping by barge that will be made possible by the four Lower Snake River Dams. Also, it would be unsound to have only one system of transportation on the river, consisting of barges, because the complex system would be very vulnerable in time of war."

"In what way will the railroad be improved?"

"Rail joints will be reduced by longer rails with a 78 foot maximum, and the cars will be made of high tensile metals. Light lock couplers, air brakes and deisel locomotives will be used."

"We have a brochure that tells how high the dams will be, how much they will cost and how our land can be irrigated from them," said Myrtle casually handing the folder to me.

As I scanned it with excitement rising in me, the pool levels, cost and power output caught my eye.

The normal pool level of Lower Granite Dam is 738 feet above sea level, Little Goose, 638, Lower Monumental 540 and Ice Harbor 440.

The estimated total cost of the Lower Granite project is targeted for $183,000,000; Little Goose, $146,000,000; Lower Monumental, $191,000,000 and Ice Harbor, $128,-000,000.

Lower Granite's hydroelectric potentiality will approximate 405,000 kilowatts with three units carrying 135,000 kilowatts each. The initial power potentiality of the completed four Lower Snake River Dams will be estimated at 1,485,000 kilowatts and ultimately 2,970,000 kilowatts.

Irrigation benefits will result from a reduced pump line to irrigable land bordering the Snake River. Availability of increased power supply will also make irrigation more feasible.

"We could increase the yields of our crops by irrigation," I said hopefully.

"Except for the thunderstorms in summer that bring heavy rain and hail, which we didn't get in the summer of 1967 for 70 days, we have only light precipitation that increases in the fall and reaches a peak in winter either as rain or snow. We can't expect snow until the middle of November or the last of it to melt before the first of March," he stated.

"Sometimes we get a 'Chinook,' a warm summerlike wind found nowhere else in the world, or a rain after February that melts the 10 to 15 inches of snow very rapidly resulting in a severe erosion of the hills and a flooding of the Palouse Rivers," I said defensively. "Frost penetrates the ground to a depth of 15 to 20 inches usually and the sun helps to break the grip of the frost."

"Are they going to do anything about the grades?"

"Access roads necessary to the construction of each dam will furnish accessibility to each of the reservoirs that will be formed behind the ladder of our dams, resulting in a succession of overlapping pools. The new roadways will lead from the main highways to the wheat developments, industrial plants, resorts, vacation homes and recreation sites —inviting boating, swimming, fishing and water sports on the Snake River," he told me.

"Where is the Boyer site for recreation going to be?"

"It will be immediately downstream from Lower Granite Dam. The access road to the Lower Granite Dam from Almota is being made 'freeway width' by earthmoving machines hauling thousands of cubic yards of dirt from the shoofly at the damsite in continuous procession toward Almota. The material is being dumped at the end and along the way to provide the roadway," Jack answered airily.

"How did the town of Almota get its name?" I asked quizzically.

"Indians were skimming the surface of the river in dugout canoes, spearing their winter food, while the green sluggish river was changing to molten silver as the rising moon glinted upon it. They called the eighty acre bar along the river, 'Almotine' or 'moonlight fishing,'" Jack hesitated and then related.

"Mr. L. M. Ringer built a warehouse on the bar in 1876 and began loading out wheat to the steamboats running on the river. After building a store in 1877, he laid out a town and changed the name of 'Almotine' to 'Almota' for it. Mr. Henry Hart Spaulding bought the land from Mr. Ringer and built the Spaulding Hotel where Mr. H. H. Selfride, warehouse agent, was the fiddler for dances and parties. In 1877, Mr. Henry Hart Spaulding became postmaster. After this, two hotels, two warehouses, a grist mill, several shops and many dwellings were erected. He turned his blacksmith's shop into a school, until a schoolhouse could be built in 1884 when forty-two pupils were attending."

I think he could see that I was restraining my curiosity, so he cleared his throat and continued, "The intrepid pioneers who lived in Almota rode their ponies or drove their wagons to Colfax over the old canyon road with its bridges made of poles. The territorial road from Dayton to Colfax, via Pomeroy, went through the town. A ferry was established in 1877, four years after the Cram Ferry was built at Penawawa."

"Jack and Myrtle Miller soon moved back to Spokane where they lived before going to Almota to live in their son's house. The 'big house' surrounded by encroaching weeds, fox tail and pennyroyal has now been torn down to make way for the port development, and some of the construction on the Lower Granite Dam has been completed.

"As relatives of the Fincher family, we were driving down to see the crumbling town of Penawawa that has been dwindling since the bridge was built at Central Ferry.

"The nearly two-hundred acres of sandy soil along the great, gray-green, writhing Snake River, which has been the home of our family and many others for a hundred years, will slip beneath twenty feet of water impounded behind Little Goose Dam," I said.

"Will Penawawa be a part of the Port of Whitman?" my daughter asked cautiously.

"Penawawa, Site No. 3, of Port Whitman, will have 7000 feet of waterfront on Little Goose Pool. Land along the river that is now under control of the Corps of Engineers will be released later to the port district. The port commission will have authority to allocate port and industrial sites," I assured her. "The Colfax Grain Growers are planning to build a wheat terminal here with funds supplied by their patrons."[14]

"Will they use the same roads?" asked Maida, my cousin who accompanied us.

"County roads 800-810, now being used for hauling grain to the Colfax Grain Growers warehouse at Penawawa for

---

14 Will Fincher, Carrie Fincher, Minnie Fincher and Floyd Loren King along with friends and neighbors will be reinterred, under the supervision of Mr. LeRoy Allen, to the Colfax Cemetery by 1969 from their resting place on the Fincher ledge at Penawawa where invading grass has healed over the scars their descent into the earth had made.

Emsley and Mary Fincher, grandparents, Johnny and Owen Fincher, great uncles, were reinterred in the Colfax Cemetery in June of 1966 with other families, many of whom were relatives.

shipping—250,000 bushels annually—will be connected to provide easy access from the farms."

"What will they do with the old territorial road?" she asked, her voice showing politeness, nothing more.

"The Penawawa road, one of the best grades on the river, is to be graded and oiled starting at Dave Repp's. Thirty thousand dollars was allocated in 1967 for this project. Seal coating of the Penawawa road for six miles will cost seven thousand, eight hundred and seven dollars which was allocated August 3, 1967," I said proudly.

"Will there be any new road?" she asked seriously.

"Six-tenths of a mile of Cr. 810 from a perspective elevator site to a point above pool level on the Penawawa Creek is estimated to cost twenty thousand," I pointed out. "Also, 1.7 miles of road which links the Penawawa Grade to the Horton Grade, a narrow plunging road along the Penawawa bar, will be replaced by the county to be reimbursed by the Corps of Engineers. This will go above the Fincher ledge, and the 160 acres set aside for the Penawawa Port Site."

"Will there be any other connecting links?" she asked, still puzzled.

"Two miles of Cr. 810 from the grain elevator site to a point above pool level on the west to the foot of the Horton Grade, now a U. S. mail route, is estimated to cost $78,000. Cr. 800 from its junction with Cr. 810 to a point above pool level 1.8 miles east of the Long Hollow will be rebuilt," I reiterated.

"When will they be taking out these once beautiful fruit-bearing orchards?"

"They will have been removed by the Harry Claterbos Company of Astoria, Oregon, during February and March of 1968," I urged.

On a return trip we noted that this work has been done but the shade trees are still standing and the portion of the old Fincher house that was the living room has been removed to the Howard Link home above the original sight to be used as a garage.

"What did you learn about the wheat terminal, Joe?" I inquired eagerly.

Joe Hodge, my son-in-law, had just come back to the house from a meeting of the Colfax Grain Growers, where he has served on the board for nine years, succeeding my husband, Will Miller, who helped to get the farmers interested in the organization and also served as a director for eight years.

"A high speed 'put through' grain terminal is going to be built on the Snake River at Central Ferry by a group of about thirty dealer grain-handling cooperatives in Whitman County and the surrounding area," he said enthusiastically. "It will have a capacity of three million bushels."

"Will the Central Ferry Bridge be replaced?" I asked awkwardly.

"The State Highway Department will relocate the Central Ferry Bridge and have now spent four months investigating soils with foundation consultants," he returned.

"How will they get to it?" my daughter Willma asked suddenly.

"A short road having a straight line distance of 3,500 feet will link the Hay-Alkali Flat road with Highway 296 near Central Ferry. It will greatly reduce the trucking distance from the south-west section of Whitman County to the terminal."

"How much shoreline will there be at Central Ferry?"

"There will be 8000 feet of shoreline on the Little Goose Pool, where the underlying cobble stones afford adequate bearing strength for construction of industrial buildings. The silt and top sandy soils are favorable for drainage. There will be 250 acres contained in the Central Ferry Site, No. 2."

"How far will the Peyton recreation site be from Central Ferry?"

"Peyton recreation site will be a few miles downstream. There will be a recreational site on the south bank in the Central Ferry Area for boat launching near the proposed Garfield County port terminal, Willow Island. Illia site will include a small park with picnic facilities."

The door bell rang and Archie Hennigar came in to tell tell us about the sale of his land at Riparia.

"How much land is the government buying at Riparia for Port Site No. 1?" I ventured to ask.

"Riparia, Site No. 1, will cover 100,000 fairly level acres that are favorable for drainage because they have 15 feet of silt or sand and beds of cobbles. The port is accessible by slackwater barge to Portland and Pasco, a graveled county highway and by the Camas Prairie Railroad," he explained.

"How much business does the Camas Prairie Railroad do in a year?" I coaxed.

"Camas Prairie moves 4,000 cars per year on the tracks from Lewiston to Riparia, with only two engines required. to move long trains on a two-tenths of one percent grade on the water level line," he informed me.

"Where was the Texas Ferry?" I asked mildly.

"Yearly packers, following the Kentucky Trail, crossed the Snake River at Texas Ferry (Riparia). Kentuckian, Joe Ruark, came to Walla Walla country about 1859 and established the trail north to western Montana and the east Kootenay country," he said vaguely.

"How big a town was Riparia?" I persisted.

"In 1882, Riparia, hit its peak with 80 inhabitants, a store, three saloons, a restaurant and a hotel," he replied calmly.

"Was there a boat landing?"

"Boats dry docked on the shores during the winter. There were two capstans and sweeps used to wind the cables. Horses were used for power. The slides were huge timbers and were greased to allow the boats to be pulled up for repairs," he divulged.

"Who operated the Ferry?" I wheedled.

"The current-powered Texas Ferry was operated by Thomas Boling. It moved wagons and stock across the river between Starbuck and Riparia."

"Why was it discontinued?" I interrogated.

"After having gone down the river when Andy Mays—an early-day resident, mounted on his horse—was riding on it, the boat went through the rapids but was picked up at Lyons Ferry; however when it broke loose during the twenties it was never recovered."

"Where is the Wilma Port?"

"Wilma Port Site No. 5 will be on the north shore of Lower Granite Pool."

"How many acres will be developed there?" I queried.

"700 acres—100 acres dotted with cobbles, sand and silt from the river bottom. The area is level and suitable for construction of the industrial buildings, storage and processing plants."

"What will the construction costs be?"

"The fixed site terminal construction costs could be from one to two million dollars."

"What are the advantages of the Steptoe Canyon Route?"

"It is the shortest route for hauling wheat from the Inland Empire to the Snake River terminal proposed at Wilma."

"What would the routing be?"

"Routing could enter the United States near Metaline Falls and follow State Highways 31 to 311 and United States 195 through Spokane, Rosalia, Colfax, Pullman, Colton, Wilma, Clarkston and Asotin to the Grande Ronde and south to Calexico, Mexico."

"Will there be passage from Wilma to Clarkston?" I interrupted.

"Yes, Wilma and Clarkston will be linked by a bridge."

"Do you know of any industrial plants that will build at Wilma?"

"Yes," he said with a grin.

"Ideal Resources will build on the land they own at Wilma."

"What kind of a plant will it be?"

"They are constructing a lime processing plant."

"When was the Port of Whitman authorized?" I asked finally. "And how much does it include?"

He sighed and then came straight to the point.

"The Port of Whitman includes the entire county area. Five major port sites will be located on the seventy-five mile shore line of the Snake River which is the southern boundary of the county. These port sites that line the waterway will be at Riparia (1), Central Ferry (2), Penawawa (3), Almota (4), and Wilma (5) for terminal development and barge transportation.

"I have a copy of the authorization in my handbook and I'll read it to you," he added.

"It was authorized under Washington State Statutes (53,04,10) to be established for the purpose of acquisition, construction, maintenance, operation, development and regulations within the district of harbor improvements, rail or motor vehicle transfer and terminal facilities, water transfer, handling, storage facilities and industrial improvement."

"Down the Snake River from the Port of Whitman a 'wheat fleet' carrying the grain from our bursting elevators will soon be gliding through the slack waters," I remarked.

He agreed.

"The manager of the Port of Whitman is Neal Klemgard," Willma reminded us.

"Is he the son of Jim Klemgard of Wawawai?" I asked.

"Yes, above the Lower Granite Dam on the Snake River, Jim Klemgard and John Metszgar, operating under the name of the Cloverdale Cattle Company, owned 700 acres of pasture land that joined the La Follette place on the east, touching the Batty property at the northeast corner and extending east almost to the top of the hill," she explained.

"Whom did he marry?" he persisted.

"After Mr. Tabor, in 1899, sold his property to his son-in-law, William L. La Follette, William and Mary La Follette invited Nora Snyder to come from her home in Allenville, Illinois to care for Tabor, Melsenia, Le Roy, Clara, Jasper, Chester and Eva La Follette.

"Nora Snyder married James Solomon Klemgard who was operating a cattle spread at Wawawai. He was reared by Peter Christianson and Lena (Kragscow) Klemgard. He had two sons, Gordon and Neal Klemgard.

"Their grandfather, P. C. Klemgaard was born in Denmark, March 6, 1821, and married Lena Klemgaard, March 3, 1856. The name was associated with Arden Parish in Jutland, England, known as Klemmegaard.

"After living in Salt Lake City, Utah, Idaho, and Marion County, Oregon, P. C. Klemgaard went to San Francisco, where he followed his trade of wagon making until 1870. Then he came north and lived on a farm eight miles southeast of Walla Walla, Washington. In 1874 he rented a tract of land in this part of the country, which he farmed successfully until 1882, when he came to Whitman County, Washington and located on a homestead seven miles southwest of Pullman."

"Would it be a reasonable assumption that Nora Snyder

was a descendant of Ann Miller Snyder's family from Berks and Sullivan Counties in Pennsylvania?" I conjectured.

"Perhaps so, as many of the younger generation were drawn to the middle states in the second migration of people in the United States," she commented.

Yesterday, we drove out to watch the cutting of our crop. As my feet slipped in the scented straw and the aroma of the fresh-cut grain permeated the air, I looked across a field of precious wheat still standing and got a feeling that I wanted to live. As the wind dips shadows in the wheat it shatters it as it has done during July of 1968. Four one hundred degree days during June shriveled the treasured heads and five very cold days in January froze it. But once again we are rewarded for our toil with a plenteous stand of Gaines—sixty bushels to an acre, 120 bushels on one acre.

Wheat—a GRASS IS GOLD to the farmer, a steward of the soil, wrought by God—is his life and breath, captor of his youth and of his dauntless soul. His heart is one with it, as was my husband's.

The sea of wheat above all other things has made it possible for the people of Whitman County to have a new hospital this year.

Later in the week I was discussing the hospital with some friends.

"When was the Saint Ignatius Hospital closed?" I asked.

"It was closed December 31, 1964 in so far as its license could not be renewed," answered Mr. Cox.

"Who is building the new hospital?"

"Bids were opened on the hospital June 6, 1967. Final approval was given on the plans by all of the agencies involved."

"Who holds the contracts?"

"ADSCO Construction Company was the low bidder on

the general contract, $756,995. Kelma-Crabtree Electric, Inc., Spokane was the low bidder on the electrical installation, $175,525, and Powell Plumbing and Heating of Moscow on the mechanical contract with $371,000. The three low bids total $1,302,520."

"Who are the architects?"

"Arnold Barton, Deeble and De Neff."

"When was it started?"

"Ground was broken and construction started in December of 1967."

"Will there be any other costs?"

"Alternate X-ray machine $40,000, auxiliary electrical generator, $10,000 and sprinkling installation about $7,000 and the paving of the parking lot, curbs and landscaping."

"How long did it take to collect the funds?"

"Two years and eleven months!"

"Will it face the Almota road?"

"The building will be placed so that the front wing of the hospital, business and administrative offices and surgery, will face the grove of trees along the Almota road and nursing wing, hospital rooms, will be directly behind. The nurses living quarters will be behind the nursing wing and almost directly in front of the Henry Savage house. The parking lot will be on the south."

"Is the building being made of all the same material?"

"The nursing wing and administrative wing are concrete and brick—no wood, completely fire proof."

'Have they received any additional funds?"

"One hundred and fifty-eight thousand has been allocated from the Hill Burton Fund. Eighty-two thousand is the amount necessary to complete the local hospital."

"Are there any special features?"

"It will have a very fine telephone service. There will be two switching consoles with telephones in three rooms for surgical patients, eight rooms for medical patients, and one room for maternity patients, for a total of twelve phones in patients' rooms. The system will have thirty-nine internal lines, five extension phones, five central office lines and one long distance line. Cost of the new service was quoted at $428 per month by the telephone company."

"Do you think heart transplants will ever be done here?"

"Twelve doctors are required."

"Visiting physicians might make it possible."

"How do they work?"

"They work in two teams. The upper chambers of the hearts of both the patient and the donor are cut off at the same place. The aorta and main chambers that lead from the heart are sutured together and the hearts sutured together. The hearts have to be the same size."

"Have any of them been successful?"

"At the Cape of Good Hope Hospital in Cape Town, South Africa, a successful heart transplant was made on a dentist, Dr. Philip Blaiberg, by Dr. Christian Barnard. Clyde Haupt was the donor and the patient made a complete decovery. Also, Dr. Joan Cogin and Dr. Ellsworth Warren of Loma Linda University of California organized heart teams that performed thirty operations in Greece."

"Are people living longer in Whitman County?"

"Yes, the people in Whitman County are slowly aging. The percentage of people over 65 years of age has been increasing steadily since 1870?"

"Why do you think this is true?"

"Improved health habits and greater medical knowledge gleaned through earnest study and diligent practices of such physicians as Dr. Frank Bryant, Dr. Paul G. Weisman, Dr. Ole Slind, Dr. W. N. Freeman, (who retired from general practice, September 12, 1968, although continuing to operate the Colfax Allergy Clinic), Dr. Robert Henry, Dr. Conrad Weitz, Jr. and many others."

"Did you know that tissues of the human body can now be frozen for future use?"

"Yes, and for a long enough time to discover a cure for the disease effecting it."

"The pace maker is being used successfully in the treatment of cardiacs."

"And life itself, indeed, have we been successful in creating it in a test tube?"

CHAPTER VIII

OUT FROM THE EARTH

As I turn the pages of my T.V. Log, I note the comments made about the events that most interested us.

"Is this the last flight of the space program?"

"Who were the men conditioned for the flight?"

"Jim Lovell and Buz Waldren were trained to walk in space on Veteran's Day. Their muscles had to be ready to make the flight."

Nelson Benton, space craft center, reporting from flight control on Agena 12, November, 1966:

"Buz Waldren to walk in space. Planes are ready on the carrier *Wasp* in case the flight has to be brought to an end.

"Count down to 7 seconds. Lift off 3 seconds after 3:45, third orbit 33 seconds long. Men wearing 33 pound black space suits and 42 pound life supports. Space belt not used. Agena lifted off in a clear clouded sky.

"Final communications check—100.6 degrees—2.17 sec. before launch.

"Tense moments—1.46 sec. and counting—1.15 secs.

"Agena back over the Cape—987654321-0.

"The capsule dives straight into the skies, gradually slanting, sputting behind. Passing out of the atmosphere 7 miles down range—10 miles altitude.

"Horizontal to 45 mi. high cut away."

Second Stage:

"7,5551 velocity 52. N. wide altitude—cut off 104 mi.

high 315 mi. down range. Engine cut off. 185 where the Agena waits for it. 6:45 after lift off."

Terry White, Gemini Control 7:53, after lift off:

"Agena trails—adjust, the phase 137 mi. by 174—mid course—160 mi. ahead over the Indian Ocean.

"9:48 66 mi. chase three times around the earth.

"Buz Waldren 36 years old. Pictures of the earth taken —yellow and black smoke ignite on being mixed with each other—propoline power—men push back in their chairs.[15]

"Booster portion falling back. Cuts off and falls back through the air. Men have been working together for five years. Stand up maneuver before noon tomorrow."
2nd day, November 13, 1966.

"We will see a man walk in space today!"

"What will he do while he is in space?"

Commentator:

"Buz Waldren standing up tethered to the capsule so he won't float away, is taking pictures of the stars. Motion toward an object pushes him away."

"When will the Apollo program begin?"

"Some time next year."

"What will our goals in space science be?"

"We are scheduled to land a man on the moon by January 29, 1969."

"Did you listen to the report from Jet Prop. Laboratory 503, Pasadena, California, in April?"

"The space craft has landing legs. The landing on the moon was perfect—speed 15 feet per second at touch down."

"It's on the moon—April 19, 1967.

"The signal lever is steady, pictures are being relayed."

---

15 Astronaut John Glenn, first to orbit the earth, Feb. 20, 1962, shares an ancestor in his mother's line with the Laughlin-King-Miller family.

"Frozen foods are being used by the astronauts, saliva from their mouths supplying the water."

"Did you know that the dry run testing of the soil from the moon will be April 21, 1967?"

"Do you think that we will find that there are men on Mars?"

"If we do should we explore the possibility of there being other stars like our world that has planets around it, that may have life upon them?"

Introduction by the announcer:

"William C. Westmoreland, Commander of Troops in Vietnam.

"Speaker McCormick, U. S. Assistant Commander in Vietnam, Mr. President, Mr. Speaker:

"I stand in the shadow of other military men here before me. I represent the fighting men in Vietnam here today. They are devoted to their mission and unbeatable in carrying it out."

"You have shown interest in the comfort and welfare of our troops."

"There has been three years of aggression from the north. For the communists strateg of war—Vietnam is a target."

"The communists sent terrorizers into South Vietnam to direct the attack."

"Their strength has doubled. Their skill is professional. The troops are well trained, bringing supplies through Laos with men on bicycles. United States has destroyed foot mobility, fugitive men, plowing materials and forced local peasants to supply food by force and evacuate dead troops."

"United States has destroyed main force units."

"Communists terrorists about 39 years of age kidnaped 26 citizens and attacked workers with grenades and gunfire, blowing bridges, blocking transportation, and bombing the source of food supply."

"Our forces have grown in strength in Thailand, Australia, Phillipines, and thirty other countries. Asia opposes Communist expansion."

"In 1954 South Vietnam had no armed forces. Vietnam's present military force is constantly growing in professional skill, three jet runways and one port for sea going ship have been built. In 1965 36,000 of the enemy were killed, 11,000 defected to the side of the government."

"Our armed forces are the finest ever fielded by our nation in this assistance to all races, creeds, and color. We will prevail in Vietnam over the communist aggressor. Fifty-eight Americans were lost in taking over five enemy lines of supplies from Laos."

"Did you know the Communists have captured one of our communications boats?"

Commentator:

"Pueblo Naval Intelligence vessel captured off the North Korean Coast by the Koreans considered an act of war. President Lyndon Johnson called up all reserves to active duty. United Nations will meet Jan. 26, 1968 to discuss this matter."

"January 29, 1968. President Johnson has demanded the return of the *Pueblo* and increased the ships and planes moving toward the area."

"It has been reported that another communications ship has been molested, February 17, 1968. The *Pueblo* is still being held by the North Korean Communists. One man who was killed or died after the capture has been returned to United States and identified by his relatives. Three other men wounded are being cared for in Korea." (All the men later returned.)

"Three flyers were released today from North Vietnam, where they have been prisoners of war. Many American soldiers are being held by the communists."

"February 19, 1968, attack by the communists on the town where General Westmoreland has his headquarters with rockets. No progress by the American Soldiers to take the communists walled up in the citadel."

"Saigon, some firing across the Perfume River all day."

"Rocket dropped on the building where the American soldiers were lined up to return home in one and one half hours. One soldier was injured by shrapnel in his shoulder another by two pieces in his neck. They were still picked up and brought home."

"Released flyers arrive home and are identified after having been reported missing in action."

"President Lyndon Johnson visited the troops at San Diego in person. The boys over there have asked for help and I know these boys will go and give them the help, as the boys over there would do if they were the ones at home."

"Communists used rockets at Hue today. Communists are walled up in the Imperial Palace. The Americans are trying to reach the citadel. Instant gas was used at Hue. Enemy may hold out a few days, from behind rows of buildings, about 200 yards to go. People are enraged by the destruction of their homes. Citadel of Hue built in 1804. The walls are forty feet thick. It was occupied by the Vietcong three weeks ago. Paintings and figurines are being destroyed, February 20, 1968."

"February 21, American flag flies over the Citadel after a 21 day battle with modern guns and barbwire blocks."

"Saigon, sixteen thousand refugees since Jan. 1, 1968. Forty percent of the houses are damaged and one hundred civilians were killed."

"February 20, 1968, Cason, waiting soldiers sing 'Where Have the Flowers Gone?' while they are playing cards at night. They jump when mortar and rockets cave in a building or a wall, between them and eternity."

"One hundred thousand men to go to Vietnam, and Americans are asked to cut down their travel in Europe."

Each day we listen eagerly to the reporting of the progress of our soldiers in Vietnam. Thus, we have a feeling of togetherness with the parents, among whom have been Mr. and Mrs. Kenneth Cain of Colfax whose son Roger Cain, 25, was the third known Whitman County Soldier lost in the Vietnam War. He was killed in action on November 21, 1967, in a road patrol unit.

September 3, 10:30 p.m., Ron Baer, commenting from the scene.

"Ten thousand years ago men who lived here were worrying about where their next meal was coming from and where they were going. Roald Fryxell and Dr. Richard Daugherty, who began in 1962 to take the soil away by hand from the Marmes Rock Shelter, one and a half miles from the confluence of the Palouse and the Snake Rivers, found two adult skeletons and one child the last week in August, 1968. These bones of Marmes man are believed to be more than 11,000 years old and the oldest to have been found on the continents of North and South America.

"There is some suggestion of a family grouping in-so-far-as arrows, weapons, and a bone needle were found in the Harrison layer.

"Dr. Henry Irwin made a scale drawing of the complex outlining the bones in ink. Elk vertebrae and ribs were battered and had series of breaks indicating that steaks were eaten possibly for ceremonial purposes or just for food. Marmes man is thought to have camped in this rock shelter as there are some evidences of a campfire and cannibalism. There would not have been enough marrow in the bones for them to have been eaten or cracked for the marrow.

"Frog and bear bones were found and the soil was sorted for the tiny bones of snakes and birds, which were examined to determine the age of the species. The bones were taken to Washington State University for further study. Shells known to be 11,000 to 13,000 years old were found in still lower layers along with flakes of bones and instruments."

"In the ice age floods stripped out the channeled scabrock and cut this canyon eighteen to twenty thousand years ago. Man occupied the area later.

"One and one half million dollars was appropriated to build a coffer-dam around the Marmes cave. Nevertheless, water seeped into the cave. It will take years to find out its wealth. Ground has been broken for a Historical Museum at the site."

"Let's see if we can get the Republican Convention of 1968."

"Where was it going to be?"

"Miami Beach, Florida."

"What day was it to open?"

"August 6, 1968."

"Which delegate do you think will have the most strength in the convention?"

"Nixon would be my choice."

"Who do you think he might name for a candidate for Vice President?"

"Hatfield of Oregon has been mentioned. Also, John Lindsay of New York."

"Wouldn't it most likely be someone who has been successful in handling some of the priorities such as housing?"

"With thirty million people in the poverty line this could be an important deliberation."

"Let's jot down the highlights of the speeches."

Ike Eisenhower speaking from Walter Reed Hospital in Washington, D. C.: "The greatness of this land is its people who are law abiding and ready to sacrifice. They are loyal and patriotic but with inflation, rising living costs, deficient currency, mounting national debt, violence and desolation in the cities, the poor are resentful and youth are rebellious."

Goldwater stressed: "This is a wonderful country we live in, and the substance of our land must not be wasted."

Daniel J. Evans added: "There is no excuse for weakness and no justifiication for lawlessness. Charity should not replace individual opportunity. We must have the privilege of making a complete study of our own needs for the Snake River Water before considering the diversion of that water into the Colorado River."

(A ten year moratorium has now been declared for this study.)

Spiro Agnew said: "The purpose of the government is not to spend money whether or not it gets the desired results. We must have equal education and job opportunities."

Presidential candidate, Richard Nixon declared: "The party that can unite itself can unite the United States. The power that has passed to Washington must go back to the states, counties, and cities. The people are good people who work, save and pay their taxes. America is a great nation and her people are great. The American people have failed because her leaders have failed. America needs leaders to match the goodness of her people. We have unprecedented lawlessness, racial violence, and fear of hostile demonstrations. I want to see it as it is and to tell it as it is. One of our first priorities is to bring an honorable end to the war in Vietnam. Peace will come through negotiations from strength not weakness. We will be as firm in defending our system as the communists are in extending theirs. We need to act like a great nation around the world. We cannot restore peace in other countries if we cannot control our own country. We must have order in the United States. We must take the law into our hearts and minds and not into our hands. The great God that helped Washington and Lincoln will help us. We need God's help and yours if we are to succeed in bringing a new dawn of peace to the United States and the world."

Dr. Billy Graham: "We pray that our choice in leadership of men, who believe in God, to deliberate the issues of our time will bring about a change in our hearts and peace at home and abroad."

"Do you think Nixon will do very much traveling?"

"He has said he will go to Russia or to Vietnam."

"He is coming to Washington and will be in Spokane so let's go up and see him."

We waited to get the 11:00 o'clock news from KXLY Sunday Evening. Announcer, Ron Baer:

"Thomas Scott on his way to Washington, D. C. from Vietnam, says the Americans want to get out of Vietnam but do not want to turn the country over to the communists. The Vietnam people must be strong enough to defend themselves, first.

"Four miles from Hue the American boys are wading waist deep in muddy water to find and bring in the enemy, mostly communists, from the water where they are hiding and breathing through straws. Air cushioned boats are being used that can go into the shallow water and over the fish weirs."

Preceding the Democratic Convention in Chicago, August 26, 1968, Edward Kennedy made his first appearance before the microphone since his brother's death. On August 21, 1968, he outlined a four point program for ending the war in Vietnam. "Cessation of bombing in South Vietnam, withdrawal of all foreign forces from South Vietnam, assistance of the United States in building a political and economic system in South Vietnam that will not collapse upon our withdrawal, and to prove sincerity a reduction of military activity in South Vietnam."

Law and order in the United States were stressed at the Chicago Convention which nominated Vice President Hubert Humphrey and Senator Muskie of Maine as the Democratic candidates for President and Vice President of the United States.

Tipped off by the postman on the porch and the clunking of the mail in the box, I slipped my T.V. Log into the rack and lay fingers on our program for the Palouse Empire Fair, September 5-6-7-8, 1968. It is held at the Whitman County Fairgrounds, a short way out in the country from Colfax, where we are going to have some fun and excitement on Saturday.

From the adjoining yellow stubble tinged with brown, a dry wheaty smell mingles with the swirling strings of dust that loop across the bumpy pasture as the mounted police at the Palouse Empire Fair motion for us to park. Strains of "Over the Waves Waltz" played by the Idaho Old Time Fiddlers lures us near the stands where the aroma of fresh, sizzling beef burgers smothered in mustard and chili sauce permeates the air. A greasy eyebrowed teller informs us, "All seats are sold out in the grandstand except singles."

"Shall we take singles, Billy?" I asked.

Billy, my grandson, has just returned from Japan where he has been serving as a communications operator in navy intelligence.

"We can get together later," he assented.

Ribbons have been awarded by the judges to the best entries in the floor show, Mrs. John Petershick, Grand Sweepstakes for a sun-washed wheat arrangement; to a best canning mom, Gladys Jefferies; the Grand Champion Angus Bull of Bill Cox's; grandmother's painting, "Lake Galilee"; for the best of grains to Dick Templeton; and the Parvin Grange for their booth, "Grain Unlocks the Door for Starving Millions."

In my diagonal, striped drip-dry jersey, I feel very confident as people are spreading down plaid blankets to cushion the dusty, splintery seats and to protect the yellow, orange, pink, red, purple and green dresses and shoes of their choice. A sailor, in white, climbs the bleachers to sit near relatives, a plane flies over the rutted field near the end where the sky lightens to an even gray and the sun is warm but not hot.

Big patches of cars emblazon the field that is flanked with yellow buses. A long line of cars—tan, green, gray, yellow and white—on the Walla Walla highway continue to turn into the pastures beyond.

The family boxes are filling up. Boys in short pants and red-candied-apple smeared cheeks are bouncing from plank to plank on possibly necessary trips.

Officials on chestnut horses ride around the arena and station themselves on a distant wind-rounded hill overlooking the grounds.

"Banjo Clown" half red, half white, and bearing up under a very large red nose has been bitten by a snake and comes to the grandstand to get a huge bottle and the announcer tells him. "Put the Seagrams Seven Crown back. Its no medicine." He appears on the stage and plays his banjo before adding an electric cord and blowing it up.

"Please get to your seats immediately, the parade will start in five minutes!" comes over the air.

On tenterhooks and leaning forward the expectant, waiting, crowd, sprinkled with mothers, glimpses a blue and white band moving toward the entrance. (Step up to let a family be seated beyond.)

"Excuse me," comes from the aisle. (Step over while a Jaycee with a gay jacket and a long shirt tail plunks down the steps.)

The thrillingly clapping crowd with glistening eyes hail the four hundred band members as they form a six patch pattern, blue and white block, Rosalia, red and black, Tekoa, blue and white, La Crosse, red and orange, St. John, black and white, Colfax and red and white, Palouse. The mass leader, Mr. Washburn, of Colfax, directs as they play the "National Anthem," "Bill Board March," and the "Cougar Conquest March," while the majorettes wave flags in the background.

A mother and her son left early so Billy moved up beside me.

"What was the last piece played by the bands?" he asked.

"Cougar Conquest March," I recall.

While the bands are marching down to accompany the floats, the colors are being raised across the field by a Scout Troop.

The American Legion Post No. 71, having their 50th anniversary, Ole Olson, commander, Tony Smick, first vice president, and Wayne Geagly, second vice president, are represented in the parade followed by the El Katif, Shriners and the Calliope.

"Who does the arranging for the fair," he pursued.

"Eva Mae Hendrickson, Inland Empire Fair President, coming in the next car is very active and the County Commissioners, Ralph Henning, Thornton, Chairman, Dist. No. 1; E. L. Harms, Pullman, Dist. No. 2; and Fred McNeilly, Colfax, No. 3, share the responsibility."

Enthralled by the beauty of each float we were the most impressed by "Drifting and Dreaming," a purple-pink one designed like a gondola with monochromatic streamers from a high square center.

"Do you think it will receive sweepstakes honors in the competition?"

"I like 'Kelly's Green' the Irish Meadow with pink-purple, and yellow flowers in high relief against a carpet of green too," I contended.

"If you like color 'Color My World,' should please you," he taunted.

The Palouse Farm family of the year, riding on the back of the beautiful gold and green Wheat Growers Association float, was passing when I noticed that Darlene Wright, a friend from Fairfield, was the Queen candidate.

"Grandpa sure loved his horses!" he commented. "Is there going to be a rodeo this evening?"

"Your grandfather used to like to lead the parade and carry the flag," I assured him. "The rodeo, symbolic of the roundups of cattle and drives to Montana markets, will have bucking contests, steer riding and a Jim Canna, which originated in Texas."

"Who has the best horses this year?"

"Owners of the best horses in the county are Jim Hayes, Colfax, Champion Quarter horse, and Calvin Parvin, Pullman, Champion Appaloose mare."

Wearing kingsize sombreros, leather chaps with deep fringe, burnished boots and loosely fitting shirts that play up their homely, yet attractive, sunburnt features, these hard-riding ranchers smile proudly as they rein up their mounts to shorten their strides and to show their best gaits. Leading the Whitman County Posse is Mike Humphrey, Whitman County Sheriff.

As we circled the booths where you try your luck at throwing for a panda doll, shooting for a green, red or yellow glass dog with shoe button eyes, or riding the whirling barrels, magnetic tractors or the roller coaster, we met John Aeschliman, my nephew, who is delighting his son, Cory, by taking him on all of the rides while Sharon and Marla revel in the artistic displays.

We turn out on the straight blacktop road that stretches across the meadow from hill to hill and cuts across alternate squares of black and gold. Decreasing moisture toward the top of the ridges is leaving a brown crop.

"What time is it, Billy?" I ventured to ask.

"Four-thirty," he acknowledged looking at his watch.

"We are to meet Willma and Joe at the Chinese Restaurant, in Pullman, at six o'clock. Do you think we can make it?"

"Travel on the Pullman highway will not be as heavy," he proffered observing the cars in front, beside and behind us.

Willma came to the restaurant door as we were parking.

"Well, I was beginning to surmise! It's a quarter after six!" she admonished.

"We stopped at Sharon's and she urged us to order seven family dinners that we could share," we clarified.

A neatly dressed waitress showed us to our six place table now stretched for nine so no one could be very expansive.

The colossal round light-green lanterns, serrated with black, hung very low over the table and gave a savory light. The topmost part of the dividers were plastic panels ornamented with triad colored chips of various sizes. A reflected light intensified the mellowness of the antique placque imported from Formosa. The red-orange leather seats wrapped their arms around us.

I was ordering a Chinese family dinner when Joe interjected, "No, I want a special steak. After all, I'm a cattleman!"

"What have Aunt Violet and Uncle Bill been doing?" Sharon asked Billy.

"They have been on a two weeks vacation to Lummi Island where they were invited to stay in a friend's cabin," he rejoined. "Bobby stayed with Jennie."

"Have Chris and Donna been home with Mark?" John smuggled in. Everyone was chatting about Violet's family.

"Incidentally why didn't you write and let us know when to expect you home?" I asked Billy.

"I was putting eighteen hours a day on a mural for my barracks," he elucidated.

"And you didn't get to keep it?"

"The Government paid for it."

"What did you do?"

"I used several of the pictures of fishwives that I saw cleaning fish in the open markets in the little village of Matsuye. Most of the stores in Japan are modern. They look like suit boxes stacked in offset piles."

After dinner we went to Sharon and John's to see their new house. Cory Lane showed us his room, and the gas station he had made in his father's shop the week-end before. We decided, from some rug samples, she had borrowed, what would be nice in her kitchen and hallway.

We came home at ten o'clock and Billy stayed and visited.

After Billy left for the Aleutian Islands to complete his last year of service, we looked forward to the flight of Apollo No. 7. We received it by radio at 7:30 A. M.

On Friday, October 11, 1968, a gusty wind is blowing as Captain Walter M. Schirra, Jr. of the Navy, third flight, Don F. Eiselle, of the Air Force, first flight, and Walter Cunningham, civilian, first flight, finish their breakfast and drive to Pad 34 where all systems will be shut down after the launch of Apollo No. 7, Saturn 1-B.

"How will they get into the craft?" I pursued.

"The astronauts will cross on the arm for installation," she interpreted.

Jack King reporting from Launch Control:

"As the twenty minute mark for launch is reached vehicle systems are being checked. 6.6 seconds hold for chill down. Go for launch, twenty months after White, Chisholm, and Chaney failed to lift off. Outboard motors shut off. Inboard motors shut off. Escape tower blows away. Schirra's heart beat 90-92. Little bumpy in the second stage."

Paul Houston at Mission Control reporting:

"They have a change of suits, room to stand up, sleeping hammocks under the seats and hot food and water."

"Apollo 7 in orbit for a planned 11 day flight of the nation's moon craft. Apollo project's first manned mission. Riding peacefully and checking."

"176 miles in orbit, orange spray in a gray sky."

"One jaw didn't deploy properly."

As we switched on the radio for the daily reports from the spacecraft in flight, I queried, "What tests and maneuvers have they to accomplish on this flight?"

"Saturn 1 B, rocket section sighted floating some 200 to 300 miles away and in a lower orbit with sextant magnification was practice in tracking objects visually; simulation or acting out of the rescue of a stranded landing crew was practiced by a successful rendezvous with the rocket hull, coming within 70 feet of it; and simulating of the rescue of the first Americans to land on the moon, consisted of a series of maneuvers and back to a rendezvous with the second stage of the booster. The lunar module will ascend from the moon's surface and use a radar system to rendezvous with the command and service module "Mother ship." Schirra will fly the Apollo 7 spacecraft as close as possible to the booster stage called the S4B, but not actually dock."

"Did anything unexpected happen?"

"Fuel supply for the thrusters ran lower than it should have, the environmental control system froze and they turned on the space radiator system to control the on-board heat, the unplanned burning of a reaction control system, and an electrical circuit failed," my daughter summarized.

"Where will they splash down?"

"Southwest of Bermuda! The Apollo 8 will circle the moon, as a result of the success of Apollo 7, and 'Out from the earth we will move!' " she commented.

Eagle, the manned spacecraft, made a soft landing in the Sea of Tranquility on the Moon, Sunday, July 20, 1969 and as this saga continues may our memories glorify the past and our vision's glow light the centuries.